LOVE, SEX & THE WHOLE PERSON

Campus Life Books

After You Graduate
Against All Odds: True Stories of People
  Who Never Gave Up
Alive: Daily Devotions
Alive 2: Daily Devotions
At the Breaking Point: How God Helps Us Through Crisis
The Campus Life Guide to Dating
The Campus Life Guide to Making and Keeping Friends
The Campus Life Guide to Surviving High School
Do You Sometimes Feel Like a Nobody?
Going the Distance: How to Build Your Faith
  for the Long Haul
Good Advice
Life at McPherson High
The Life of the Party: A True Story
  of Teenage Alcoholism
The Lighter Side of Campus Life
Love, Sex & the Whole Person: Everything You Want to
  Know
A Love Story: Questions and Answers on Sex
Making Life Make Sense
Next Time I Fall in Love
Next Time I Fall in Love Journal
Peer Pressure: Making It Work for You
Personal Best: A Campus Life Guide to Knowing
  and Liking Yourself
Welcome to High School
What Teenagers Are Saying about Drugs and Alcohol
What They Never Told Me When I Became a Christian
Worth the Wait: Love, Sex, and Keeping the Dream Alive
You Call This a Family? Making Yours Better

LOVE, SEX & THE WHOLE PERSON

(Everything You Want To Know)

Tim Stafford

A DIVISION OF CTi

CampusLife / ZondervanPublishingHouse
B O O K S / *Grand Rapids, Michigan*

A Division of HarperCollins*Publishers*

Love, Sex & the Whole Person
by Tim Stafford
Copyright © 1991 by Campus Life Books, a division of CTi
All rights reserved

Campus Life Books are published by
Zondervan Publishing House
1415 Lake Drive, S.E.,
Grand Rapids, Michigan 49506

Library of Congress Cataloging-in-Publication Data

Stafford, Tim.
  Love, sex, and the whole person : everything you want to know /
  Tim Stafford.
      p. cm.
  "Campus Life books."
  Summary: Questions and answers with a Christian perspective about
love and sex have been compiled from columns in "Campus Life"
magazine.
  ISBN 0-310-71181-9
  1. Sexual ethics for teenagers—Miscellanea—Juvenile literature.
  2. Sexual ethics for youth—Miscellanea–Juvenile literature.
  3. Sex—Religious aspects—Christianity—Miscellanea—Juvenile
literature. [1. Sexual ethics. 2. Christian life.] I. Title.
HQ35.S736   1991
306.7'0835—dc20   91–2512
                                                          CIP
                                                          AC

All Scripture quotations, unless otherwise noted, are taken from the *Holy Bible: New International Version* (North American Edition). Copyright © 1973, 1978, 1984, by the International Bible Society. Used by permission of Zondervan Bible Publishers.

Edited by Gerard Terpstra
Interior design by Ann Cherryman
Cover design by The Aslan Group, Ltd.

Printed in the United States of America

91 92 93 94 95 / CH / 5 4 3 2 1

About the YOUTHSOURCE™ Publishing Group

YOUTHSOURCE™ books, tapes, videos, and other resources pool the expertise of three of the finest youth-ministry resource providers in the world:

Campus Life Books—publishers of the award-winning *Campus Life* magazine, for nearly fifty years helping high schoolers live Christian lives.

Youth Specialties—serving ministers to middle-school, junior-high, and high-school youth for over twenty years through books, magazines, and training events such as the National Youth Workers Convention.

Zondervan Publishing House—one of the oldest, largest, and most respected evangelical Christian publishers in the world.

Campus Life
465 Gundersen Dr.
Carol Stream, IL 60188
708/260-6200

Youth Specialties
1224 Greenfield Dr.
El Cajon, CA 92021
619/440-2333

Zondervan
1415 Lake Dr., S.E.
Grand Rapids, MI 49506
616/698-6900

THANKS

This book is gleaned from over fifteen years of questions and answers in the pages of *Campus Life* magazine. My column, "Love, Sex & the Whole Person," first began through the insistence of Harold Myra and Philip Yancey, who worked with me at *Campus Life* and have been wonderful friends and co-workers since. I owe them a great deal, and I owe them for this.

A number of people have served as my editors at *Campus Life*: Gregg Lewis, Steve Lawhead, Verne Becker, Andrea Midgett, Kris Bearss, Jim Long, and Diane Eble. I am thankful to them all for guidance and for friendship.

I am especially grateful to my friend Lesley Van Dordrecht, who read carefully and thoughtfully through fifteen years of material—much of it repetitive—and selected the best of it. Her skillful labor has made this book possible. Her husband, Mike, also read the work and made helpful suggestions.

Finally, I must thank my wife, Popie, who is the single best reason why I am still enthusiastic and idealistic—in fact, more than ever—about sexuality as God intended it.

—Tim Stafford

Contents

3. Controlling Sex in Relationships

4. How Far Do We Go?

5. Why Wait?

6. Masturbation

7. Homosexuality

1. Dating/Relating

I'm shy, and I've never been on a date. How do I ask a girl out?

Q: I have a problem: I'm twenty-three years old, and I have never been on a date. I know there is nothing bad about being single, but I want companionship. I'm shy, and I don't know how to ask a girl out or what to do on a date. Could you please give me some advice?

A: Unfortunately, there is no quick cure for shyness. If there were, I'm sure I would have discovered it. I spent a lot of years being very shy.

Some things help, though.

1. *Concentrate on friendship, not romance.* Try to make some friends, male or female. Learn how to walk up to someone and, after introductions, ask questions that get a response—questions like, "What do you enjoy doing?" or "Have you seen any good movies lately?" Learn how to listen to what someone is saying, rather than just talking about what you're interested in.

2. *Start small.* If you're afraid to single out a girl and ask her out, ask a dozen people out. That's called a party.

And rather than trying for the big Saturday-night outing, try for a little after-work Pepsi. Try for brunch after church.

And rather than thinking about the busy, happy,

friendly girls, try to think of the girls who are more or less like you—shy and not very outgoing. Believe me, they are interested. I know, because every time someone like you writes in, five or six girls write in telling me the Lord instructed them to ask for your address.

3. *Hang around the places where the kind of people you like congregate.* You're aren't going to meet people sitting at home. Get involved in something you genuinely enjoy.

4. *Try, and keep trying.* You are going to look stupid some of the time, but I guarantee that you won't look nearly as foolish as you think you will. The truth is, most people are so busy worrying about what kind of impression they're making that they don't have time to worry about whether you look bad. After a few dozen failures, you begin to realize that the world is still spinning, and nobody is walking around laughing at you. In fact, most people are sympathetic to someone who's willing to try.

5. *When you don't know what to do or what to say, try smiling.*

For me, it was helpful to develop a "let's get it over with" attitude. I realized that as long as I gave in to my fears, I'd be miserable. But as soon as I did what I dreaded—called a girl up, for instance—I felt better. Even if I got the dreaded rejection, it was better than worrying. It was like going to the dentist with a sore tooth. You dread it, but the sooner you go, the quicker you get relief.

I think he likes me. How can I get him to ask me out?

Q: Recently I started praying for a Christian boyfriend. Not too long after that, Scott came and sat next to me at the table in art class. I have always known that he is a really nice guy, but I never really knew him. Scott talked with me about all kinds of things. That happened a few days ago, and ever since then he has sat next to me in art. We always talk to each other a lot.

I have really grown to love him. He is so kind, so friendly, and has such good Christian morals. I am pretty sure that he likes me, too, but maybe just as a friend. My problem is that I would like to have a boyfriend-girlfriend relationship with him, but I don't know how to get it started. He either is too shy to ask me to go out with him, has never thought about it, or doesn't want to go out with me. What can I do to get a boyfriend-girlfriend relationship going between us?

A: You have several options: (1) You can ask him out. This takes some nerve but in most cases has the desired effect. (2) You can invite him to do something in a group—for instance, a fancy dinner party at your home. This is more subtle but often works. (3) You can write him a letter or send him a message through a friend that you really like him and wish you could go out together. This leaves the initiative to him, though it is clear enough that you are really the one making moves. (4) You can continue being friendly and hope he gets the idea.

Which option you choose probably depends on how brave you feel. I see no harm in letting a guy know you're willing. Rarely does a guy resent this. It isn't necessarily easy for guys to put their egos on the line and ask a girl out. Most guys—especially shy guys—are happy to know in advance that their interest is welcome.

Yes, I know it's tough to take the initiative. How do you think guys feel? But the more initiative you take, the more likely you are to succeed.

How do I turn someone down without hurting his feelings?

Q: I've known Rich for about three months now. He's part of a group of kids I'm in, and a lot of times we all go out together for coffee. I like him as a friend, but I think he has a crush on me, and I just don't feel that way about him. We've gone out a few times, and the last couple times he's called up I've begged off. Once I really was busy, and another time I had an excuse. But I could sense he was disappointed.

I like him and don't want to make him feel like he's repulsive. But I would also like him to know that I don't feel romantic about him. How can I?

A: As a guy, I've gotten that word a few times in my life, and I can testify that there's no painless way. If you really like someone, it hurts to be told the feelings aren't mutual, no matter how it's done.

I've known girls who have strung it out so long they would hardly tell me when I asked point-blank, and I've heard it from girls who let me know, subtly or unsubtly (and usually only the second kind works on me), on about the second phone call. I know for sure which I prefer—the second way. It hurts for a while, but you're not so involved you can't get indignant and forget it in a few days. The longer you wait, the harder it is to get over it.

Try something like this the next time he asks you out: "Rich, I'd like to go out with you, but I don't think it's a good idea. I like you as a friend, but I'm just not ready for any kind of romantic attachment."

I'd tell him, too, how you feel about saying that. Tell him you've been afraid he'd take it wrong, but you decided he'd be able to understand how you felt without thinking it had anything to do with not liking him.

Don't expect miracles. It will hurt him. Sometimes the

kindest thing, though, is to hurt someone a little—so you won't have to hurt him a lot later on.

How can I have great communication with my date?

Q: In a recent column about avoiding sexual temptation, you said it was good for couples to ask themselves, "When did we last have a great conversation?"

What do you mean? Would you please give some examples of great conversations? I want to keep my relationship with this guy fresh. I never want us to get bored with each other.

A: A great conversation involves the hearts and souls of people. It's not just enjoyable, it is intimate. Through it we learn to see each other better, as though from the inside.

It is impossible to establish rules on "how to have a great conversation." Different subjects excite different people, and everybody has his or her own style of talking. But good conversation follows some general patterns:

1. *Good conversations are two-way*, with both parties listening and talking.

2. *Good conversationalists don't just rattle on with news or views.* They reveal their inner selves, their thoughts and cares and interests.

3. *Good conversationalists listen carefully.* They ask good questions, trying to see into the other person's heart and mind. They don't just hear the surface, they try to hear *under* the surface.

You don't want to grow bored with each other? Then learn how to converse thoughtfully. Couples who communicate well don't get bored with each other, not in a thousand years. They find endless fascination in learning more about the person they love. According to some "experts," the art of love is knowing how to perform well at sex. But the art of communication is far more important. It never gets old. It provides food for every other area of life.

We're talking but not communicating. How can we build our relationship?

Q: I have a different kind of problem. I started going out with this girl about five months ago. It was really looking great in the beginning, but soon vacation came and we really didn't see much of each other (only at church events). We talked a lot on the phone, though.

Now we're on the phone a lot, but we're not talking. We don't talk much when we're together. They say communication is one of the most important things in a relationship. I really can't see much communication in ours. Don't say just go over and talk to her because it's harder than that. Please answer because I really want to make this work.

A: Your letter is different, all right. Not that others don't share the problem of poor communication; about 95 percent do, I'd guess. Few confront it, though, as you want to. You're making a good beginning just by asking the question.

Males and females are attractive to each other—that's a biological fact. They don't need communication for that. They can feel excited just looking at each other. Many relationships therefore "look great in the beginning."

As you're discovering, however, males and females are also very different. Bringing two unique people together in genuine love requires that they try to understand each other—

understand the differences as well as the common ground. That takes communication. "Great feelings," "comfortable silences," "having fun together"—these are no substitute.

But few people are naturally good communicators. Communication is not the same as talking a lot. It has more to do with listening carefully. To communicate, you must explore new ground, not just make noises about the things you've been doing. Communication requires that you put into words the ideas and feelings you've always taken for granted—those ideas you thought everybody shared, but which your partner doesn't. Communication is, therefore, hard work for most people—as you've discovered.

Let me tell you first what not to do. When two attractive people can't find anything to say, they're tempted to fill in the silence by getting physical. Making out does cover the embarrassment and leaves a feeling of becoming closer. It never substitutes, however, for communication, and if you try to make it a substitute, you will wreck your relationship. You may "stay together," but your love will grow hollow instead of growing fuller and deeper.

Communication is a skill to be learned. There are no magic secrets, only practice, practice, practice. As in learning basketball, you feel awkward at first. You just have to keep practicing until it begins to feel smooth.

Here are a few hints that might help you:

1. *Keep your practice sessions short and frequent.* It's usually better to talk every day for five minutes than once a week for two hours.

2. *Carry a notebook during the day and jot down thoughts you'd like to communicate so that she can understand you better.* Keep track of feelings, opinions, and conversations that come up in the events of the day. Then, when you talk, just go through the list. Get her to do the same.

3. *Learn to ask opening questions and follow-up questions.* You can jot these down in your notebook too. "What did you do today?" is a poor question. "What did you do in basketball today?" is a mediocre question. "How does the basketball

coach act in practice?" is a better question. "What is it about basketball that you like?" is another.

4. *Share spiritually* by telling each other what you learned from the Bible (no matter how small) and by praying for each other in specific ways about activities and problems you have told each other about. Then you're not just communicating to understand each other; you're communicating in order to help.

How can we develop a spiritual relationship?

Q: I have a question that I'm sure is universal. How do you begin developing a Christian relationship with your boyfriend or girlfriend? I mean, I know it begins with both being Christians—but where do you go from there when you're not used to sharing something so special and private?

I love the Lord with all my heart and want to grow in him with my boyfriend. But this is new to both of us, even though I've been a Christian for twelve years. I'm not used to worshiping with anyone else. My boyfriend and I live far apart. (I'm in college; he's in the army.) It'll be two years before we can get married, so we have all the time in the world. Gary (my boyfriend) is in agreement with me, and I know that he'd appreciate help also. I can't talk to my pastor or parents, because, as I said, I'm in college. We're praying for guidance, that's all I know to do now. Do you understand where I'm coming from? Any help?

A: If two people are sincere believers, their faith in Christ is bound to permeate the way they treat each other. I believe this must be true with you and your boyfriend. More than you realize, you are developing a Christian relationship.

LOVE, SEX & THE WHOLE PERSON

However, I think I understand the problem you express. You want to learn how to talk about your faith together, how to encourage each other, how to pray together, how to openly share a part of life that is very deeply personal. That's a worthy goal.

For some people it comes easily, whereas for other people (usually more private personalities) it's extremely difficult. I don't think there's a cookie-cutter approach that works the same way for everybody. But I can share a few ideas that might work for you:

1. *Tell each other about the Christian activities you do separately.* Since you're apart, you can't usually share the same experiences together. But you can read the same Christian book or listen to the same Christian cassette and then discuss it through letters or over the phone. Each of you can keep a spiritual journal and then talk about it with each other. Both of you can agree to pray for the same people or concerns and encourage each other to persist in these prayers. Both of you can study the same biblical passage each day and write each other what you learn from it. These exercises may seem stiff and formal at first, but if you keep at them long enough, you'll learn to understand and appreciate each other's spiritual life more.

2. *When you're together, attend church together.* Then compare notes about what you learned and experienced.

3. *Try to develop the habit of talking about your life in Christ when you're together.* Talk about what you've been doing and learning and what areas you feel weak in.

4. *Pray together.* If it's too difficult to pray out loud, then pray silently and tell each other afterwards what you prayed about.

If you both love the Lord and want to grow in him, you'll want to talk about that with each other. There's no "right way" to go about it; these are just some possible activities that might help you develop a natural style. It doesn't have to happen overnight. Take your time but keep looking for opportunities to open up spiritually with each other.

I'd like to drop my boyfriend for another guy, but I'd feel guilty.

Q: I have a boyfriend I really like, but I also like a friend of his. His friend flirts with me some, and I flirt back when my boyfriend isn't looking. This makes me feel guilty. I think I'd drop my boyfriend for his friend, but how do I know if he's just teasing me? I'd feel really guilty about dropping my boyfriend. I think I still care for him, but the feelings are being transplanted. How can I stop this? Or should I stop it?

A: What you should stop is the games. It's okay to stop liking one person and start liking another. The mistake is pretending and flirting behind someone's back. That's called hypocrisy. It's a very poor foundation for building any kind of friendship.

That's why I have a problem with "going steady" as it's usually practiced. It's natural, if you really like someone deeply, to prefer his company all the time. But often "going steady" becomes a system that forces people together whether it's their natural tendency or not.

Going out is meant to offer you some experience in forming friendships with the opposite sex. You can get over your shyness and awkwardness and find out a little about how to act when romantic feelings enter the picture. You defeat the purpose of going out if you try to make it into a premature marriage, an arrangement by which one person is strictly "tied" to another and can get out only through a big, emotional breakup.

Your best bet is to talk to your boyfriend and tell him you still like him and would like to go out with him—but that you also want the freedom to go out with other guys. He may not like that, but if he really cares for you, he'll want you to feel as free as you want to be.

You're not married yet. Don't continue the mistake of "playing" marriage.

Is it okay to date or even marry a person of a different race?

Q: I am twenty years old and white. I met a twenty-two-year-old black guy through a Christian fellowship on my college campus. After getting to know each other, we discovered that we had a lot in common and that we had very strong feelings for each other.

I've lived in a white neighborhood all my life. To me, people are who they are inside, not according to their outward appearance. So it was easy for me to look beyond this man's race. Little did I know this attitude would cause such problems.

When I came home one night and explained to my parents the relationship that I had with this guy, my calm parents became hysterical in a way I had never seen before. They forbade me to ever see him in a dating relationship. They reacted out of fear for me and, I believe, for themselves also. They said if it led to marriage, that we would have too many problems because society doesn't accept it. I felt the right thing to do was obey them and pray for their attitude to change.

A few days later they apologized for their reaction and said that it was my decision, but they made it perfectly clear that they disapproved. I then began to see him again. My parents and I didn't get along very well during that time, and eventually they cut off almost every possible way that he and I could meet or talk—even though they had said it was my decision.

My parents and I have always been very close, and this turmoil at home became almost unbearable. If this guy didn't mean the world to me, I would say, "It's just not worth it." I'm not rebelling against my parents; I really love them and want to please them. I find myself having to choose between them and the man I love.

His parents and family love me to death. This type of relationship is not unfamiliar to them. I have had no problems dealing with his race. He has grown up in the white world and some of his best friends are white. I've been told that I am naïve. I really don't know the problems that I may face, but do I run from everything that looks difficult?

Then there is the controversy of children. Is it fair to them? How different is having a race-mixed child from having an albino or an extremely ugly child? Many children go through teasing while growing up.

My main concern is to do God's will. Right now I'm not sure of what that is. Do I look for God's will in my parents? My parents are devoted, strong Christians, but they are only human. They tell me that this relationship will hurt my witness as a Christian. What do you think?

I've searched the Bible for answers but find nothing about interracial marriages. Abraham told Isaac not to marry a Canaanite but one of his own kind. He did this not because of race but because of the wickedness of the Canaanites. Can this be related? Ephesians 6:1–2 says to obey your parents. Does this mean all your life? I am twenty but still living under their roof and dependent on them for my college education. Romans 10:12 says there is no difference between Jews and Gentiles. Are these different races? Does this have anything to do with marriages?

I am a Campus Life staff volunteer and have led some small groups on dating, love, sex, and marriage. I have some strong ideas and am very picky when it comes to choosing a man. As far as the person is concerned, this guy is right for me. But all the pressures are confusing me. I know all things are possible with God. He could have another man out there who is white and just as wonderful. But if this black man is God's will for me, then what? Would God allow my parents to disapprove if this relationship were his will?

A: It's natural for parents to feel sick at heart when they see their daughter headed toward a lifetime of struggle—unnecessary struggle, as far as they can see. Your parents are right about the views of society. The hysteria you've observed in them is a sampling of the hostility and suspicion interracial couples can feel in America—not from everybody but certainly from some. Underneath the cool surface a great deal of racism hides. I think it's getting better, but it's still very strong. An interracial couple would do well to take a good, long look at that before they make any decisions. A lifetime is a long time.

Apart from that, you are free. The Bible says nothing about the right or wrong of interracial marriage. Race is simply not a factor. As you note, in the Old Testament Israelites were warned against marrying people from other nations, but this was a concern about their faith, not their race. When people from other nations decided to follow the God of Israel they were fully accepted. Ruth, for example, was a Moabite, but she not only married into Israel, her great grandson was David. Clearly neither she nor her offspring were treated as second-class citizens. The New Testament makes this crystal clear: all distinctions of race and nationality mean nothing to Christ. When Paul wrote that in Christ there is neither Jew nor Gentile, he was talking about a prejudice between cultures that was, if anything, stronger than the modern-day prejudice between black and white. In Christ, such distinctions mean nothing.

Could God's will be against your parents' will? Certainly. If your parents were thieves, it would not be God's will for you to steal. If your parents sexually abused you, it would not be God's will for you to submit. If your parents are still bound by the sin of racism, it is not God's will for you to be bound by the same sin. The command to obey your parents is always conditional, even for the smallest child. Wrong doesn't become right because your parents say so. Jesus plainly predicted that families would be split over his message, and his prediction has proved true many times over.

That doesn't say you are morally obligated to marry this

man. It just says you are free to decide. You will need to consider your parents' feelings very seriously, as you would for any big decision. Their adverse reaction is a "fact" that you have to consider. All through your life you will owe your parents honor, and at least while you're under their roof and dependent on them, you owe them obedience in every possible area. I think you should try your best to do as they say, even if it puts your relationship on hold for a while. Ultimately, however, I believe it is not right to bind any person's freedom because of racial prejudice.

Is it right to fall in love with and marry a person of a different denomination?

Q: I have a very special person in my life and that is God. He is with me every day and helps me through everything. Except I have one thing I have become very confused about. I have a relationship with a man whom I really love, and I feel God has made him for me. Our relationship has survived many downfalls, but there is one problem I have yet to understand. Both of us love and believe in God, but he is a strong Catholic believer and I am a devoted Lutheran. We do love each other and have discussed a possible "forever" relationship although we are afraid the religious differences may cause problems. What happens to our children? He says he wants many children and that they will be brought up as Catholics. I guess I would like my children to be Lutheran. But does it really matter how we label our religion? As long as we all have Christ in our hearts and believe him, trust him, and serve him—can't it work? Will this be a big problem for our relationship? If so I'd like to know what we can do to deal with it.

A: You're right when you say that a relationship with Christ is more important than your denominational label. You'd have a far better chance for a successful marriage with a genuine believer from another Christian church than you would with a fellow Lutheran whose faith is meaningless.

Still, the differences between Lutherans and Catholics are deep. Although doctrinal differences stand out far less than they did fifty years ago, they still exist. It may be that neither of you is very concerned with doctrine, but even if you could put all doctrine aside, many practical differences in how you live your faith still arise.

The biggest practical difference is that the Lutheran church and the Catholic church are situated on different corners. Even before children enter the picture, you must face the choice: Where will you go on Sunday morning? If you are really "one" in marriage, you won't want to split up to worship God. If you go to each other's churches on alternate Sundays, the practical result is that each of you is only half-way committed to his or her own church. There is no good compromise, so far as I'm aware. We live out our love for Christ in fellowship with a specific group of people. A married couple need to do that together.

The only real solution is for one of you to give in completely to the other—or for both of you to choose a new church altogether. That's a difficult solution, one that most Christians find much harder in practice than in theory. I wouldn't put this choice off until the wedding day. Face it now, or say good-bye. Make sure you understand all that your choice implies. Talk to your own pastor and to your family members. Get all the information possible before you plunge.

The way you face this dilemma will tell a lot about whether or not you and this man really are "meant for each other." For if you are really meant for each other, I am sure you will both be able to joyfully worship God in the same family of believers. And if you can honestly face this problem, you'll be able to face others.

What about dating non-Christians?

Q: I am a senior in high school. My boyfriend is a junior, and we have been going together for about two weeks. We really hit it off great together. I am a Christian, and though he isn't, he doesn't drink, smoke, take drugs, or go for sex before marriage.

But my mother gave me this big lecture about going with him. She thinks something is going to happen (like becoming pregnant). He told me that one of his sisters became pregnant before she was married and he never forgave her, so I know he doesn't believe in it. We don't plan to get serious because I will be going on to school (about a hundred miles away) and he has two more years of high school. We are just going together for this year. Do you feel there is anything wrong with going with him?

A: That depends on what "going with him" means. If, consciously or unconsciously, you're thinking about getting seriously involved, it's a problem.

You say you don't plan on that, but the emotions of love can sweep you into something that will hurt you both—and I'm not talking about pregnancy. I'm referring to a deep bond of love when one party doesn't have an inner relationship with Christ.

There's certainly nothing wrong with going out on a friendship basis. It could give you a chance to help him become a Christian—the greatest thing you can do for anyone. And a strong friendship—any really genuine friendship, no matter with whom—is a precious thing.

The trouble is, very few people go out strictly on a friendship basis. Somewhere in the background is the hope for romance. Even if you are not planning on becoming involved, love has a way of making its own plans. Many,

many people have started into a relationship telling themselves it's "just casual." They ended up deeply in love, and then they were faced with a truly terrible dilemma. Either they could go on and marry someone they could never share their faith with or they could break apart from a person they truly loved. I wouldn't wish that dilemma on anyone.

That may be a part of what's in your mother's mind. Also, I wouldn't underrate her concern about sexual involvement. Just believing that sex before marriage is wrong isn't enough: lots of unmarried mothers and fathers believed it was wrong. We all have a strong sexual drive. You have the strength of Christ to resist temptation. Your boyfriend doesn't. His reasons for being against premarital sex—and his scruples about all the activities leading up to it—may be very weak.

Another problem with dating a non-Christian is the potential for losing contact with other Christians and ultimately with God. This can happen in very gradual, subtle ways. Perhaps your boyfriend takes up a lot of your time, and he doesn't want to go to church. First thing you know, you're too busy to pray or spend time with other Christians. You're not reading the Bible. Naturally, you feel lost and lonely. But instead of turning to God and to other Christians, you turn even more to the guy. You stop talking to him about Jesus because your relationship with Jesus isn't too great. Subtly, without planning it, you drift very far away from God.

For most people, going out with a non-Christian is a bad idea. There are exceptions, and perhaps you are one of them. But I think you'd be better off listening to your mom.

I'm already in love with a non-Christian. What can I do?

Q: I've been reading your column for a couple of years, and I have your book *A Love Story*. In both you've dealt with the question, "Is it wrong to date a non-Christian?" and said, basically, yes it is. I suppose you get a lot of "Well, what if . . ." questions. Here's another. I can understand why you say we shouldn't marry non-Christians, and I respect your opinion. It makes sense, but. . . .

Well, I met a young man, "Jim," about three years ago. I was not a very strong Christian at the time and was going through some really tough personal problems. He is from another country and had never heard about God before. But we went to church together, and some other Christian friends talked to him about Christ. He listened but was not totally convinced, and he is still struggling with the idea of believing in God, the Bible, all of it. But he hasn't totally dismissed Christ as a legend. It's very hard on him, not being sure one way or the other.

Soon after we first met we became very good friends. He stood by me through my problems. Three months later he went home. We kept close in our letters, and I soon realized I was falling in love. That year, I rededicated my life to God and have led a very Christian life since, or tried to.

A year ago Jim came back and spent two and a half months here. We began dating, and a very strong love grew between us. When he left, he promised to send half of the plane fare after I graduated, so that I could go and visit his home. We write regularly and our relationship has grown even closer. We haven't talked about getting married, but he says he has thought about it, and I know I have.

When we were dating, I had no idea what the Bible said about marriage to non-Christians. I asked God to guide our relationship. Jim stopped drinking for me, and when the subject of sex came up, he was as opposed to the idea of premarital sex as I was. I've gone out with some Christian guys, but none can compare to Jim and how I felt when I was with him.

Now it's too late to deny my love for him, to forget about him, or to be just friends. It's very hard to be apart, but it would be harder to stop loving him. What should I do? I don't feel like God is telling me to break up.

A: One point of clarification: I don't believe dating non-Christians is always wrong. I think if you're looking for friendship, such dates are fine. But when the real agenda isn't friendship, but mate-hunting, such dates become very doubtful. I haven't met many people who could say, with all honesty, that their deepest interest was simple friendship.

You're a good example of the subtle problems that dating non-Christians leads to. Non-Christians are not bad people. They may be very fine people. Only one quality sets all non-Christians apart from all Christians: they have not decided to follow Jesus. The difference this makes may not be very obvious. But God has posted a warning: someday it will mean the difference between life and death.

Knowing this difference, the Bible commands that Christians and non-Christians not be "yoked" together (2 Corinthians 6:14). Why? When two animals are yoked together, they must both pull in the same direction. But by definition, Christians and non-Christians are headed in different directions in the most basic issues in life. It is a kindness to Christians and non-Christians alike not to yoke them together. Married people who are going in different directions will pull and haul against each other. They end up going nowhere, and they keep rubbing sores on each other in the process. Ask somebody who's tried.

When you're married, you and your husband become partners, establishing a life together, serving others together, probably raising children together. Qualities that didn't seem terribly significant while dating become drastically important then. Basic values come out. Any non-Christian has decided one basic value: that Jesus Christ is not of ultimate value to him, and he will not build his life on Jesus. That will clash with a Christian's values at many, many points.

You're in a spot. You can't go back to being "just friends"—at least, not painlessly. But you can't painlessly go ahead with your relationship either. You can carry on the relationship, but where will it lead? Ultimately you have to choose whom you want to make the foundation of your life. Will Jim be most important, or God? If it must be Jim, then

God will be in second place—a position he does not function well in.

But if God, what then? Then you will be communicating to Jim the strongest witness any person can make to another. You will be saying to him, "I love you; I want to be your partner, but something else matters so much to me that I will do without you if you will not share it with me. God matters more to me than you."

There is a possibility that this witness will convince Jim that your testimony is real. There is a possibility that your stand will open the way for him to follow you in faith. God's reality becomes clear to many people only when they see Christians acting as though God is real.

That is a possibility. But there is no guarantee. If you cannot make this stand, however, something quite different *is* guaranteed: Jim will never learn the meaning of commitment to Christ from you.

I don't envy you this choice. It will be hard. I trust, however, that through God's power, your witness, and Jim's sensitive spirit, the end result will be far, far better than you yourself could ever have designed.

How can I sensitively say no to a guy because he's not a Christian?

Q: I am a moderately attractive Christian girl and last year I was a freshman at a state community college. Early in my teens I made a decision to date only Christians and not to get romantically involved with any guys who don't have the same commitment to God. In high school I seldom socialized and made few friends, so guys hardly ever asked me out. However, in college I fit in more easily without compromising my standards. I am much happier and have become popular with a lot of nice people.

Now my problem is how to refuse dates with non-Christian guys. I've wracked my brain for a polite way that doesn't insult them, but so far I've just managed to stutter eloquently. Once or twice I tried to explain my view as a Christian, but the response was an indignant, "What do you mean? I'm a Christian—I used to go to church." A simple "No, thank you" might work but doesn't express my appreciation of being asked nor explain that I'd rather not be asked again. It really hurts to always have to say no, especially when the few Christian guys I have ever been interested in never went beyond greeting me in church.

Is there a way to decline invitations without sounding mean or like a religious snob?

A: It's obvious that your attitude is good—that you are not acting from pride or false holiness. So the problem is to get that across. It's not easy. By the time a guy works up nerve to ask for a date, he is usually edgy, primed for rejection. He wants a yes or no, not an explanation.

Would you feel comfortable with this? "Thank for asking. I feel good that you did. But I don't feel free to go out with you. To explain why would take time. It has nothing to do with liking you. It has to do with my faith in Jesus Christ. I'd love to explain it to you over coffee, if you'd like."

I doubt you can get your point of view across on the phone, at least during that tense moment. And some guys, let's face it, aren't going to be interested in understanding your point of view. But at least suggesting a meeting should also let any guy know that you don't dislike him.

Of course, I realize that your counter invitation may confuse the guy, but if you mention Jesus, most guys will at least suspect they're not in for romance! In this situation you have a wonderful chance to share your faith in a practical way. The guy can see that you're serious about what you are saying, and he knows it makes a difference in your life. That can be powerful!

Should I date someone a lot older than I am?

Q: I am a fifteen-year-old sophomore in high school. I've been a Christian since I was a kid. My problem is that I enjoy the company of college-age guys whom I have met on Christian retreats more than high school boys. All the high school guys I know do not want to talk—they want action. I would much rather talk about Christianity with "older" guys.

My mother says that I should stick to guys my own age. But the ones I'm interested in are either not interested in me or interested in me for other reasons. One counselor at a retreat I attended told me if I were in his college I would have more dates than I could handle "because college guys are interested in more mature qualities." I don't want to wait three years for guys my age to notice these qualities in me. Should I continue corresponding with and seeing my college friends—or look closer to home as my mother suggests?

A: I don't think there's any right and wrong to this, and it certainly won't do you any harm to have older friends. There is, however, something to the idea that a person can grow up "too fast." You can force tulips to bloom early, but I understand they bloom for only one season.

I'm sure your heart sang when that guy told you lots of dates are waiting for you in college. It is exciting to be with older, more sophisticated people. But those older friends will never be in your situation, facing your problems. When you're in college, they'll be out working, getting married. When you start your first job, they'll have been working for years. You'll never be the same as they are.

I would suggest, then, that you don't give up on guys your own age. If they seem to lack interest or only want "action," it could be because they don't know yet how to carry on a conversation. But they can learn—at least some of them can. You don't have to cut off older friends. But make sure your friendships don't exclude your own peer group, where you can form relationships that are relevant to the pressures you face, and where you'll really be an equal.

How can you have a relationship "long distance"?

Q: I met this really neat guy at camp last summer. I write to him quite a lot, and he faithfully responds. I have grown closer to him through each letter. We have written for about five months now. My question is, can you actually grow to learn so much about a person through letters that you begin to develop a true love for him?

A: I don't know any rule that says you can't. Some people date for a year and learn less about their partner than you can put on a postcard. So you aren't necessarily lagging behind.

But most of the time letters don't express a very large slice of the whole person. He probably doesn't write you about his faults very much, for example. He surely doesn't describe the nervous habits he has that may, in person, drive you nuts. When he writes, he locks his attention on you. In person, his interest may wander. There are simply a lot of things that don't come through in a letter.

That just means you need more than letters for love to develop into maturity. The question you ought to ask, before you let yourself fall in love with him, is, "When are we going to get that chance?" It's a sad thing to hear from people who have dreamed up romantic schemes with someone they don't know very well. Their castles usually end up crashing down. If you have the choice, it's better to invest in someone you can see.

I'd never suggest you stop writing, but I would suggest you work at developing relationships with people who are closer to home. At this point in your life, you don't have to choose. You can have both.

Can you keep a relationship going when you're separated by thousands of miles?

Q: I'm an eighteen-year-old guy with a fifteen-year-old girlfriend. She's absolutely the best thing that's happened to me, and I've been able to help her, too. In fact, she became a Christian recently after struggling with the decision for more than a year.

Too soon, though, the big test is coming. I'm joining the navy. I'll be in for four years, and I'll only see her every few months. We love each other very much and seriously consider marriage after the navy. Right now, though, we both have a lot of growing and changing to do. What I'm worried about is that we'll grow away from each other while I'm gone. We know we won't be able to go steady while I'm gone, but we do want to do whatever we can to strengthen the relationship. It scares me to think what might happen.

A: To strengthen the relationship you can pray for each other, and write often. When you write, don't dwell on your relationship—that kind of romantic dreaming can get very old after a while. Instead, work at sharing what you're thinking about, the people you're meeting, the things you're learning. Concentrate on keeping her familiar with the real you, as you change and grow.

You will change. Neither of you could stop changing if you wanted to. Keeping current on those changes through letters at least gives some hope that your relationship can continue. It can't continue the way it is.

Will it change for the better or for the worse? Will you grow closer or farther apart? Only God knows. This is an area where you simply have to trust God. He wants to give you the best. If your relationship is really the best for you both, then no four-year separation could be too much for him to overcome. On the other hand, if the relationship doesn't hold over the separation, I'd take it as a sign that God has something better he wants to give you both.

Therefore don't cling to the past. Be glad for the love you've had together but, trusting God, hold it out and let him take it. He may give it back, better than before. He may give you something better in exchange. But he will most certainly not give you something worse.

2. Breaking Up/ Brokenhearted

How can I stop loving someone after we've broken up?

Q: Four and a half months ago my girlfriend and I broke up. It was and is one of the hardest things I've ever had to deal with. I loved her very much and, though it's unfortunate, I still love her. It's unfortunate because she evidently doesn't love me.

Since then, I have dated other girls, but I just can't stop thinking of her and wishing I were with her. She is now going with someone else and seems to be getting serious.

For so long I thought everything was all right between us. But after she broke up with me, I started feeling harsh and bitter toward her, especially when she started going with someone else. I tried completely avoiding her—not even speaking to her. Doing this not only hurt her, it hurt me. I can't turn around and just be her friend the way we were before we went out. It's not that simple. I don't know what to do.

I love her and can't have her. We never had sex together—we knew that would be wrong. How do you stop loving someone you can't have who still means so much?

A: You don't stop loving her. Time brings the loving to an end—you don't. Eventually the feelings fade, and life goes on. Until then all you can do is avoid hurting yourself—and her. Here are some suggestions:

1. *Don't pay her back.* She's hurt you, and you feel natural anger. But avoid acting out those bitter feelings. From her perspective, she may have good reasons for calling it quits. You may someday live to thank God she dropped you. One thing's for sure: nobody will be better off if you make her sorry. It doesn't rekindle love.

2. *Give yourself some space.* Feeling as you do, you can't be her closest friend. Don't try. Maybe you could write her a note explaining how you feel. Tell her that you need to stay away from her, just for your own emotional stability. Then do so. Give her a chance to live her own life, and give yourself the same chance.

3. *Don't isolate yourself.* You probably don't feel like talking to anybody, but make yourself be around others. It's natural to want time to think and stew as part of the grief process. But make sure you stay in touch with other people. Give them a chance to be your friends. Don't nurse a grudge against the world. Don't fantasize yourself as the world's Loneliest Man, or that is what you may become.

4. *Don't fall in love for a while.* There's a phenomenon known as "falling in love on the rebound." People who have been dumped often jump into some other relationship very suddenly, as though making up for what they've lost. These relationships can develop high intensity very quickly, because people on the rebound try to make up for the last relationship by jumping to the same level of intimacy in the new relationship. Such relationships often end in much deeper pain and sometimes permanent damage. When you're emotionally unstable, it's easy to build fantastic skyscrapers of cardboard, which quickly topple over in the first wind.

You should be thankful you didn't have sex with your girlfriend. Although your wounds are deep, they are clean, and they will heal cleanly. You have nothing to be ashamed of, only much to be sad about. Life is full of sad events; you can't avoid them. But you can avoid things to be ashamed of. They not only hurt; they cause damage as well.

How do I deal with the loss of my boyfriend—and the guilt I feel over our sexual involvement?

Q: About one year ago my boyfriend and I decided to put Jesus first in our lives. Then after about two weeks my boyfriend was being teased so badly that he gave up. I wanted to keep trying. Eventually we broke up.

I was really hurt because I love him a lot. We got back together and broke up again about a month after having sex. It has been about four months since we broke up, and I still love him a lot. But I have a bad feeling of guilt. I was changed after having sex with him. (I was a virgin before then.) Everyone is telling me to forget about him, but I don't know how. I feel so close to him. How can I get over him? How can I get rid of the guilt feelings?

A: A lot of people know just how you feel—and wish they didn't. A cocktail of bad feelings—of regret, of lovesickness, of guilt and shame—make you sick at heart. It just won't go away. You wonder if you'll ever be happy again.

You will, but only after time has worked to blur all your memories. There's no shortcut through this grief.

God has provided a shortcut through the guilt. In 1 John 1:9 is this promise: "If we confess our sins, he is faithful and just and will forgive us our sins and purify us from all unrighteousness." You've confessed, and so you can live through this with Jesus rather than without him. He gives hope. His message is that you can truly recover.

You are not going to pay for your sins. Instead, you are going to be rewarded with everything heaven and earth have to offer. Jesus himself will never leave you; he will accompany you on your journey to a destination he has chosen. Read through Romans 8 and see whether there is anything in your experience that can separate you from Jesus and his love.

But why, then, do you have to endure this grief? If God can reverse sin, why not the feelings of guilt and regret?

I'd suggest that what's beating on you is one of the laws of the universe. When you love someone, and particularly when you sleep together, you're bound together. You can never lose those vivid memories of being together. Indeed, you'll have them if you live to be a hundred. The ghost of your boyfriend is still with you. And part of you is missing; it's with him. No wonder you feel bad.

People who come together sexually are not meant to ever come apart again—at least, not for long. But you gave yourself, body and soul, to a relationship that didn't have the strength to hold together. Maybe it will help you, as you go through this, to know that the same strong feelings will work in your favor, someday, if you marry.

While you wait for your grief to fade, use the time to strengthen relationships. You have a choice—to push others away and isolate yourself, or to allow others deeper into your life. Often deep friendships are formed during times of deepest sadness. Often, too, a deeper reliance on God grows.

It hurts so much.... How can I go on?

Q: I've known this guy at church since I was five years old. I've liked him since I was ten, and finally at age fourteen he asked me out. (I know at this point you're probably thinking "circular file," but please hear me out.)

It seemed to me like the perfect relationship. I mean, think about it: he is the hunk of the youth group, a great Christian, and I like him! He boosted up my very low self-image and brought me a lot closer to God. He started coming over every day (my mom won't let me date for another year and a half, which I think is reasonable) after work. We'd swim in my pool, and we'd have a great time.

This went on for about a month, and then everything just stopped. No phone calls, no visits, he wouldn't even talk to me at church. After about a week I finally got ahold of him, and he just said it was over. He gave me a *very* vague reason, and I was so shocked. What did I do wrong? From then on I've been awful. I'm a jerk when I'm with the youth group. Every time after I see or talk to him at all, I just cry and cry when I get home. We've been broken up for three weeks. You're supposed to forget by now, right?

My mom just makes my life more miserable. She hates him, and yells at me if I should even look at him. The killer of the whole situation is that three people that he has talked to said that he said he still likes me but the time just wasn't right.

I'm just so confused and so hurt. I obviously can't talk to my mom. My pastor, forget it, you'd have to know him to understand. I've prayed about it, but it's just . . . I don't know. Since he left me my self-image and my relationships with God and a lot of other people have gone down the drain. I don't want to write, sing, or socialize any more. I'm just torn apart inside. Please, I'm getting really desperate. I've been playing around with suicide. I just want an answer. And if you knew me, suicide would be the last thing you would expect from me.

A: I don't think you need help from me nearly so much as from somebody nearby. You need someone to go through this sad time with you. It's often true that the most lively, sociable people lack a really close friend. That may be a reason you fell so hard for this guy—and felt so desperate when he left.

Have you really dropped your front and tried to communicate to someone how awful you feel? If you haven't talked to someone, it's possible nobody has any idea. It's hard for them to help when they don't know how much help is needed.

Naturally, you want to know what went wrong. Was it your fault? Was the guy simply a jerk, as your mom seems to think? My opinion is that it probably wasn't anybody's fault. Emotions run wild when you're trying out love. They can change in a minute, for no good reason. My guess is that the guy gave you a vague answer because that's all he had. For some reason, which he might not have understood himself, he grew restless and uneasy, and he just had to get away. The feelings may switch back just as quickly. Or they may not.

Of course, he dumped you without the politeness of a gentle explanation. Would that have made it easier? Maybe not much. But he certainly owed it to you. With Christians love isn't all or nothing. We retain a steady commitment to love, whether or not we stay boyfriend and girlfriend.

But often you both need some space, some distance to let emotions cool down. He should have done it differently. But now that it's done, he may be doing you a favor by staying away. Talking might just make you feel worse.

What do you do now? Go ahead and cry. It won't hurt you. Try to get a friend to cry with you. By all means, *talk to someone about your fears of suicide*. I'd strongly suggest a trained counselor. And go on about life. Try not to misbehave too badly in public—you don't need any more problems than you already have. Pray. And wait. Three weeks really isn't very much time to heal a broken heart. When you care about someone, you can't forget him overnight.

But you will forget him, in time. Sometimes it takes a lot of time, but the healing comes. I promise.

How do I break it off without hurting him?

Q: I have what I consider a serious problem. I met this guy (he's really nice) last year at a youth conference. He asked me for my address, and he gave me his. I took it, knowing I'd never write unless he wrote me, and of course he wrote!

We became really close. He took me to Prom; I took him on youth-group trips, I was even introduced to all of his relatives. (ALL OF THEM!)

But then I left the country for a three-month mission trip. Before I left I thought he was the only Christian guy who was living a Christian life. This summer I met over fifty guys who were all living Christian lives. I wrote him (my boyfriend) and told him I didn't want to go any further in our relationship. Well, he wrote back, as I knew he would, and said, "But you've done so much for me I feel I owe you for all you've done!" and "But you're the best thing that's happened to me. I LOVE YOU!" His sister tells me I am the first girl he's ever said he loves. But I can't help that. I tried to tell him nicely that I just want to be friends, if that. Then he writes back and calls me and has the same thing to say. How do I tell him I don't want to see him without saying, "DROP DEAD!"?

A: That is a serious problem. Some guys don't get the message easily. And let's be candid: You took a very sudden U-turn. He's still going 65 mph in the old direction. It's not easy for him to suddenly stop loving you just because you wrote him a letter.

That's the risk of love: it can hurt. You can't stop it from hurting.

You can limit the pain, however. A clean break is better than a tortuous farewell. You've made the right first move. Now how do you get him to accept it?

All you can do is repeat your message, firmly and clearly. Say everything positive that you honestly can. Tell him that you like and respect him, but that so long as he is thinking about romance an attempt at friendship will be doomed. Tell him that you both need time to let the emotions cool and for that reason you don't want to see him for a good long while. Then, if he keeps on calling, just stop talking to him. Say goodbye and hang up.

I hope it won't come to this. But if he won't get the message, don't try to reason with him. Just quit responding. Don't take his calls. Don't answer his letters. It may seem heartless, but it's not. It's realistic. In the long run it will make the break easier for him. He needs to stop thinking about you and start thinking about others. He also needs to learn to listen when a girl says no.

If we got back together, could it be different?

Q: My question is pretty quick and to the point. My boyfriend and I recently broke up. Only, we still care about each other and miss each other. Is it possible for the relationship to be wrong but not the person? Also, if the person is wrong, how do I get him out of my mind? I don't want to forget altogether, but sometimes he seems to dominate my thoughts.

A: Yes, it's possible for a relationship to go wrong even between two people who are "right" for each other. In fact, that's what often happens. The partners fall into patterns that bring out the worst in each other. For example, acting jealous and possessive, taking each other for granted, letting sex dominate, permitting one person to control (or even abuse) the other, or relating on a superficial basis. The most compatible couple in the world can fall into such traps. And they do, they do.

People put too much emphasis on finding the "right one." They're constantly asking themselves or their friends or God, "Is this the right one?" They act as though getting the right answer will guarantee a successful romance. But it won't. Compatibility helps, but a relationship that's deep, loving, and intelligent requires more than just a good match. It takes work, wisdom, character—and usually the help of God.

You and your ex-boyfriend may be, for all I know, a perfect match. I'd warn you, though, not to jump back together too quickly. If you do, you'll probably make the same mistakes all over again. Something went wrong. Use this lonely time to get perspective on whatever it was. Then ask yourself, Do I really want to do what's needed to fix it? And does he? Will he?

If the answer is no, then your last question becomes important: How do I forget him? You may not like this answer, but it's reliable: Give it time. Grieving over a broken relationship is something like grieving over a death. There are no shortcuts. You have to simply live through it. The more you cared for him, the more it hurts to lose him (even if the relationship was a mess). You can't make the pain go away. You can't even hurry it up. You can just wait. The pain may seem to last forever, but it won't.

Still, you're going to think about him for a while. I hope those thoughts, painful as they may be, lead you somewhere. I hope that the next time you fall for someone you'll be older and wiser, instead of merely older.

3. *Controlling Sex in Relationships*

How can we avoid giving in to our sexual urges?

Q: I'm sixteen, and so is my boyfriend. We've been friends for about eight months and started going out a little over three months ago. He's a wonderful Christian guy and we both love God very much and want to please him in our relationship. The question is how.

A few weeks ago we first messed up. We went a little too far but fortunately stopped early. We were only lying on each other. But the next weekend we went a little farther, and the next a little farther. We stopped as soon as we realized what we were doing. After each time we both felt incredibly bad and talked about it at length. And about our pasts. Both of us have made some mistakes, I with an old steady boyfriend and he before he committed his life to Christ. But we're both miraculously still virgins. I really believe God protected us both.

So now what's my question, right? It's how. How do we make it the next four to six years before we marry each other or someone else? We really need some practical ideas. Can you help?

A: I think so. Your problem may seem enormous to you. To me it sounds manageable, for one simple reason: you want to manage it. It sounds to me as though you both sincerely want to keep your sexual drives under control. If you want to, you can.

It's when people have mixed feelings—when they want to stay out of bed, but not too far out of bed—that I'm not hopeful. Or when one partner is for control, but the other isn't. God made sex to be powerfully attractive, and if you aren't sure how you want to direct it, it will set its own direction. It's like damming the Colorado River—you can do it, but don't try to do it in a half-hearted way.

Controlling your sex drive, by the way, isn't a skill you need only before marriage. It's important for married people too. They have to learn to focus their urges in a way that serves the purpose of their love. For example, how do they handle it when someone else attracts them sexually? Or how do they handle it when their partner is sick, or pregnant, or too depressed to want to make love? A lot of marriages fall apart because one or both partners never really learned how to control their desires for the good of the relationship.

Now to get practical: the two of you need to sit down and decide why you are dating. Talk long and honestly about the goals of your relationship. Then talk honestly about the kind of date that will serve those goals. Talk about physical contact and how that will serve your goals.

For example, one reason people date is to feel secure. They like to know that somebody finds them attractive. For them a good-night kiss may be a symbol that this is a "real date." Without it they might feel as though they were going out with their brother or sister. They may agree that a good-night kiss is part of a date. It serves the goal of reassurance. It communicates attraction. But they don't have to spend forty-five minutes kissing to fulfill that goal.

Other reasons people go out together are to get to know each other, to learn to be comfortable around the opposite sex, to encourage and strengthen each other, to have fun, and to find out whether they are meant for each other. To accomplish each of these goals, some activities are appropriate, and some are not.

When you've talked about the philosophy of your

relationship, you should set some standards. What do you believe should happen on each and every date? What should never happen on a date? What ought to happen on at least half of your dates?

A sample list might begin like this:

1. On every date we should learn one new thing about each other.

2. On at least half of our dates we should spend an hour or more just talking. We will keep up to date on each other's family, school, friendships, and activities. We will work at understanding each other's family background. We will share our spiritual growth.

3. Since we want to be involved with friends together, we will spend at least half of our time with other people—family or friends.

4. We want never to spend more than five minutes at a time just getting physical. Five minutes is plenty to express what we want to express.

5. We want never to touch each other in areas that clothes normally cover. We think that's unnecessary and will only make us wish for more.

Don't rush into setting standards. Really talk about them, and make sure you both agree. Write them down together, and from time to time review and update them.

I think a lot of people get overly involved physically because they don't know what else to do with their time. They're excited about being together, their hormones are bubbling, they're not really very comfortable talking—so they do what feels good and takes no skill. But developing a good relationship is a skill, and it takes conscious effort. That's why I'd say that the positive standards are just as important as the negative. You need agreement not just on what you won't do, but also on what you will do.

I'm not going to suggest that sex will stop tempting you. If you're normal, you'll feel sexual desires. Other desires, however, can be stronger—the desire to develop a relationship that you can be proud of, for instance. It's obvious from your letter that the two of you are just drifting along, doing what comes naturally. If you keep drifting, the current will carry you away. You need to set a positive direction. Whether you someday marry or not, it's possible to form a relationship that will leave a positive mark on both of you for the rest of your lives.

I'm afraid I can't resist temptation. Where can I find strength?

Q: After dating several girls off and on, I finally became serious with a girl in twelfth grade. We dated for about five months and then she told me she wanted to make love to me. I truly regret I ever let her talk me into it. This sexual closeness lasted for about a month, until her father found her birth-control pills. I was really sorry I had been living in such sin. I confessed and asked God's forgiveness. The relationship ended a month later.

Now I'm afraid of dating a girl more than a couple of times because I'm afraid the same situation might arise. To tell you the truth, I'm afraid I might fall back into the same sin if I'm pressured enough. Yet I do want a girlfriend.

I happen to know some girls who are free with their bodies, and whenever I get depressed I think about calling them. But I never do. My problem is that instead of calling these girls, I masturbate. After doing this, however, I feel so guilty that I forget completely about calling anyone. I'm not sure if masturbation is wrong; all I know is that it stops me from falling into sexual sin.

A: Maybe so, but there are surely better ways to fight temptation than making yourself feel so guilty you forget about it.

Your biggest mistake seems to be fighting temptation totally on your own. When the pressure has invaded your mind, fighting alone doesn't work very well. Nor will it work to avoid getting close to girls. Sooner or later you'll cave in, because temptation will wear you down.

Jay Kesler has pointed out that there are two ways of coping with pressure. One way is illustrated by bathyspheres, the miniature submarines that are sometimes used to explore the ocean floor at a depth far greater than an ordinary submarine can safely go. At the bottom of the ocean, the pressure from the water is enough to crush a conventional submarine like an aluminum can. So bathyspheres prevent that by having plate steel several inches thick. Unfortunately, this makes the bathysphere very heavy and difficult to maneuver. They have to be kept small, and there's hardly any room to move inside.

However, when the people in the bathyspheres descend to the bottom of the ocean, they find they are not alone. They turn on the lights and peer out of their tiny, thick plate-glass windows, and what do they see? Fish!

Fish cope with extreme pressure in an entirely different way. They don't build thick skins. In fact, they remain supple and free. They compensate for the pressure through equal and opposite pressure inside themselves.

What you need is something inside you to equal the pressure of temptation. For Christians, God's Holy Spirit wants to provide that. But how do you bring him into operation?

First, you pray and read God's word. But don't do it alone. God's Spirit is not given in full power to sole individuals. It is given to his people, worshiping and praying together. Look through the book of Acts in the New Testament, a book that some have called the Acts of the Holy Spirit. Almost always at least two people are working together for God; often you see a whole group in close fellowship when the Spirit comes on them with power.

This applies to temptation also. I've rarely seen someone

resist great pressure strictly alone. The power over sin, which God gives, he gives to a fellowship of Christians.

This means you need to find at least one other person—and preferably a whole group—with whom you can share your struggles. But it doesn't end with sharing. You need people who will pray for you, and people who can counsel and encourage you from God's Word. It's amazing how much equal and opposite pressure such a group fellowship brings against the pressures of the world around you.

Next, and just as important, you need to get to know girls who love life so much they have their bodies under control.

There are plenty of girls of this kind around. Some would love to meet a guy who isn't dominated by sex. Maybe the groups you're in aren't like that. If so, think about changing groups. Some girls, like some guys, aren't going to put you under pressure. They're going to be on your side, helping you resist temptation. Most probably, when you find a group that will pray for you and encourage you, you'll find girls like this in it. Their attractiveness will counteract the attraction of the girls you're tempted by now.

Is it possible to "back up" in a sexual relationship?

Q: I was reading an answer you gave to a question about "proper sexual conduct" on a date. You said that petting can only be harmful. You are 100 percent correct. My boyfriend and I just broke up after three years of going out. One of our problems (we had quite a few) was that we had gotten too physical. Although we never made love, there was quite a bit of "everything but." I don't feel guilty about anything, but I do wonder if what we had between us was real.

What my question really is, I guess, is that assuming

that it was real at one time (it was for me and still is), is there any way of going back to how things were without the physicalness? Is it possible to pick up the pieces after something like this? We are still really good friends and I still love him very much. Can the past be forgotten and ourselves controlled?

A: Yes, it's possible to start over, though it's never easy. The habits of "getting physical" are strong. Most people, once they've tried something, find they can't stop. That's one reason I often tell people there's no such thing as sexual experimentation. It's like experimenting with pregnancy. You can't just decide you made a mistake and go back to the way things were before. The way out of your mistake is much more complicated than the way in.

Lots of people find it's easier to break up than to start over the right way. Yet some people do manage to begin anew. If you're people of character, you can. Here are some recommendations I'd make for doing so:

1. *A lengthy cooling-off period can help.* How long? Let's say, for starters, three months.

2. *You and your friend ought to spend most of your time with other people, not alone.* If you need to talk privately, go to a coffee shop. Learn to get as much pleasure from talking together as you got from touching each other. (It's possible.)

3. *Try going out on your first date all over again, and get it right this time.* If you think all a couple should do on their first five dates is hold hands, do that and no more. It won't feel natural to start over again, but then, what did "feeling natural" ever do for your relationship?

4. *Take the time to talk at length about "getting physical" and what your plan will be as you start over.* Talk about what you want to be off limits and what you need to do to keep inside your limits. Talk honestly about what leads up to temptation. Usually there's a whole train of events that become almost irresistible. Trying to stop the train after it's gained speed won't work. You need to stop it early. It will

probably be difficult to talk about this honestly. It's easier to just set some standards and hope you can keep them. Hope alone isn't good enough, however.

Can this strategy work? It really depends on how much you want to make it work. Are you willing to put up with all this unpleasantness? Is your relationship worth it? You'll have to decide for yourselves.

How can we gain sexual control, after we've lost it so many times?

Q: I've been dating a new Christian. In fact, I'd dated him before he became a Christian. When the relationship led to petting, I couldn't control the situation. I prayed a lot and finally decided to break off.

Now, some time later, we're back together. I'd decided to cut off the sex completely except for a good-night kiss, but it didn't work. We've talked of marriage; I'm out of school now, but if we're not mature enough to handle sex, I can't see how we'd handle marriage. Now when I'm with him, I don't care what we do. The only time I feel bad is afterwards, when I realize it's wrong and I should have enough love for God to do what's right.

This summer I felt depressed and alone. Seeing him is all I live for. I try to do what's right. I pray, but then I hate myself. I have only one person to talk to. Please tell me what to do. I'm going crazy.

A: Reading your letter, I was struck by the fact that you never mention what your boyfriend thinks about all this. I can't believe you left that out by accident; I'll bet you haven't honestly discussed things (not just sex, but your whole relationship). I am sure of one thing: you won't solve the problem by yourself. Even with two of you working on it, it would be very difficult. If, when you talk about it with him, your boyfriend can't see the importance of changing things, or even if he says he does but won't work at restraining himself, I'd advise you to break it off. You'll never succeed alone.

The change can be made, but it will take a whole new approach to your relationship. I'd like to quote from a letter I got recently:

> In a recent issue you told two Christian kids to be creative in their relationship, so not so much "free time" is left open. I just wanted to share what my fiancé and I have discovered in this area of our relationship.
>
> We both feel premarital sex is wrong. But . . . where to draw the line was becoming more and more difficult. We both were feeling guilty and often said, "We've got to quit." Finally at Christmastime God really put the thumb on us, and we came before him and asked for his help—his power. It was like a ten-ton burden was lifted! We set limits: no lying down, no petting at all. We tried to think of ways to be creative in expressing our love. We're still learning, but here are a few ways that we've found bring intense satisfaction—much more than we've ever found from frustrated and unfulfilled physical expression.
>
> 1. He gave me a rose for no special reason.
> 2. We've written poems for each other. We've also just shared classical poetry, love poems by the great poets. Sometimes they say what you're feeling, but could never express.
> 3. Singing to each other.
> 4. Shopping together. Any couple who can shop for four hours together without getting grumpy or irritable has definitely learned a lesson in getting along.
> 5. Working on hobbies together.
> 6. Spending time with other couples.
> 7. And the most exciting thing we've found is really praying for each other.
>
> Sharing in other ways now will make our sexual relationship after marriage so much more precious.

Before God turned us around, I'd never thought much about an actual sexual experience—just kind of got carried away in "how good it felt" to pet. I never wanted to do the real thing—I was scared. Now I'm anxiously waiting for sex. God has changed so many attitudes since we surrendered to him.

I know now that if you really want to love a person you have to be willing to be a bit frustrated at times, and come up with a creative alternative in order to be in a place where God can pour out his blessing in full on the relationship.

I like her letter particularly because it shows that controlling sex doesn't mean you turn off sex. She claims more appreciation and anticipation of sex—not less.

One other important note: please realize God forgives you. You aren't helping yourself by hating yourself. In fact, the guilt feelings probably drive you steadily into more failure. God is not pleased to see you hating yourself.

Everyone fails, and nearly everyone experiences guilt at some point in life. The incredible, marvelous thing about being a Christian is that we have forgiveness. There are no strings attached. You cannot sin more times than God will forgive you.

Most misuses of sex come as a result of reaching out for love in some way, I think. Experiencing God's loving forgiveness will help fill that void in your life—and reduce the motive that drives you back into petting.

Talking to a pastor or a strong older Christian can be a great help in experiencing this forgiveness. Hearing someone say, "I forgive you, and God forgives you" puts flesh and blood to what you know in your head. I'd recommend you go to such a person and ask point-blank, "Do you forgive me? Does God forgive me?" You need to hear the audible answer "Yes. I do. He does. You are forgiven."

What if my boyfriend is out of control?

Q: My boyfriend and I are both Spirit-filled Christians. I don't mean to make him out to be the bad guy, but he does give me problems. Always, when we are sitting close together, he wants to touch me where I don't want to be touched. I have to be on my guard constantly, and keep pushing his hands away. I know that hurts him, but I try to keep high morals and I just don't want him touching me like that. I tell him he should fight those desires, but it seems he doesn't even try. He even tries to take my hand and force me to participate.

I don't know what to do. We've prayed about it a lot. I've pointed out some Bible passages I thought might help, but the only response I ever got from him was, "The Bible says it's better to marry than to burn." I don't want to get flustered and angry about this. We are very patient with each other and have not even quarreled in the four months we've been together. Can you give me some advice on what to do?

A: Maybe you should quarrel a little. If your boyfriend acts the way you say he does, you've got something to be flustered and angry about. You say he is a Spirit-filled Christian. Is this the same Spirit whose fruit includes gentleness, patience, and self-control? Maybe a little more filling is in order.

But that's your boyfriend's problem. Your problem is that you've been willing to put up with him. He is not treating you like a human being but like an object. He probably is nowhere close to being ready for a mature relationship. But you are encouraging his immaturity by tolerating him.

It's time for a confrontation. Read him what Galatians 5:22–23 says the Spirit produces in a person's life. Tell him that his actions don't stack up. Set a clear boundary for his hands and tell him when he goes over the boundary the date is terminated and you won't see him for two weeks. Then keep your word. He just might get the picture and grow up. More likely he won't, and the termination will be permanent. You'll only be losing a headache, though.

Looking back on my own life, I can wish that a few girls had been tough with me. I hope I never acted so immaturely as your boyfriend, but I did have my problems. Immaturity isn't cured by soft, half-hearted pleas, any more than pleading makes a naughty child stop putting his hand in the cookie jar. The clean slap of discipline does a lot to help people grow up. I'm not the only guy who can look back and wish he'd had a little more of such discipline.

4. How Far Do We Go?

What does the Bible say about how far you can go?

Q: I am a nineteen-year-old college freshman. Throughout high school I dated guys very steadily and have continued dating here at college. All my relationships have been serious and committed, and entirely with Christian guys. But no matter who I date and no matter what occurs sexually, I find that the same question arises: What is proper sexual conduct?

I am still a virgin, and I intend to stay a virgin until I'm married. My friends and I have tried to find references in the Bible concerning proper sexual conduct outside of marriage, but our efforts have been unsuccessful. How far is "too far"? I've been in situations where I wasn't sure what was right or wrong. This issue is very rarely (if ever) addressed. Could you please give me references to reflect on? All I want is to keep God's will in every area of my life.

A: In the period in which the Bible was written, there were no "teenagers." When young people reached puberty, they were adults. They didn't date, they didn't kiss, they didn't worry about premarital sex—they got married. It isn't that there weren't problems, it's just that the problems were different.

In those days, a guy didn't have to worry about how far to go with his girlfriend. He didn't *have* a girlfriend. He seldom even talked to girls his age. Nor did he have the frustration of waiting for marriage: he married, in all probability, not long after the age when sexual feelings began to come.

That doesn't mean he was problem-free. He may have been terribly tempted by prostitutes, for example. There were even religions that used prostitutes for part of their worship.

We have different problems—at least they're different on the surface. And kids twenty years from now will face problems different from yours. If the Bible tried to solve all the problems of all ages, it wouldn't fit into any library. It would be too long.

That's why the Bible doesn't precisely answer the question, "How far should I go?" What the Bible gives us is better anyway. It gives principles. It tells us what's really important in life.

Here are some of these principles that can help in deciding how far you should go:

- You shouldn't do anything on a date that you will feel ashamed of on your wedding day. Hebrews 13:4 states, "Marriage should be honored by all, and the marriage bed kept pure. . . ." You need to think about how your actions will affect you tomorrow— particularly when and if you marry. You want your marriage bed to be "pure," meaning uncontaminated.
- You should do only what is truly good for both of you. Hebrews 10:24 says, "Let us consider how we may spur one another on toward love and good deeds." Whatever you do together ought to encourage both of you to become better people. If you eventually marry, you will want to remember your courtship as a period in which you grew spiritually. If you eventually split up, you will want to remember your relationship as one that left you both better people. When you ask, "How far is too far?" you must ask not only what's wrong with a particular activity, but also what's right about it. How is it helping you both to grow?
- You should avoid sin at all costs. Colossians 3:5 reads,

"Put to death, therefore, whatever belongs to your earthly nature: sexual immorality, impurity, lust, evil desires and greed. . . ." Ephesians 5:3 puts it this way: "Among you there must not be even a hint of sexual immorality, or of any kind of impurity, or of greed, because these are improper for God's holy people."

Some people want to go as far as they possibly can without quite going over the line. That's not the mentality the Bible teaches. We're taught to be uncompromising in our attitude toward sin—to stay far from anything that's questionable.

The answer to your question, then, comes from examining any activity in the light of these three principles. Does it honor your future marriage possibilities? Does it build both of you up? Does it keep you from sexual impurity? If the answer to those questions is no, then it's "too far."

Please be specific. How far is too far?

Q: My question is one that many unmarried guys like me are wondering about. It is the basic question of what is "legal" and what is "illegal" while a couple is dating. I have heard many conflicting things from youth group directors, parents, other dating couples, and my Christian friends. Of course, everyone knows that today's world says, "If it feels good do it, as long as you don't hurt anyone else." But what does the Word of God say?

A: I have to admit I don't like the words "legal" and "illegal" applied to this question. They sound like speed limits—and everybody knows that when you know the speed limit you drive at precisely that speed, or a little faster. Your only concern is negative—not to get caught. I think the answer we need is a positive one.

This problem didn't arise in ancient cultures where there was no dating and where the sexes were largely segregated until marriage. So the Bible doesn't give specific guidelines. But some Bible verses give us an idea of the attitudes we should have. In 1 Timothy 5:2 Paul instructs Timothy to treat younger women as "sisters, with absolute purity." Some people think that means you should never do something on a date that you wouldn't want to do with your own sister. But I wouldn't even want to go on a date with my own sister. I think a better contemporary reading would be: Don't do anything on a date you wouldn't want someone else to do with your sister.

Another relevant passage is found in Romans 12:9–10, which says, "Love must be sincere. Hate what is evil; cling to what is good. Be devoted to one another in brotherly love. Honor one another above yourself."

This passage wasn't written particularly to male and female friendships, but it reminds us that the qualities of Christian friendship should be part of any romance: sincerity, devotion, respect, honor, and a deep desire to avoid anything that even hints of immorality.

Applying this is something else. One difficulty is that the same action can mean different things to different people. For some cultures, a kiss is a very intimate thing. For others, it is a way of saying hello.

So how can you decide? In addition to the principles I have already offered, I suggest you ask two positive questions. First, what do we have to say to each other? And second, how can we say it?

In a casual relationship, you may not have much to say in physical terms. Even holding hands may be too strong for the light affection you feel.

But no matter how deep a relationship is, the most you can say to each other is this: "I love you very deeply. I am serious about you."

And how, physically, do you say that? Here is my view, for what it's worth: before marriage, everything I needed to express physically was expressed adequately in a fairly brief and tender kiss. After that, trouble began.

When I went beyond kissing, I was expressing something all right, but I have doubts about whether it was something good. It's been my experience and the experience of others I've discussed this with that an evening of sweaty and slobbery wrestling is not a particularly helpful kind of communication. It ends only in frustration.

I think kissing is a good limit. I recommend it. But I would be wrong to say that that is what God's Word recommends. There are Christians who think that kissing is going too far, and there are Christians who think it is quite all right to go considerably farther. Nobody can impose a limit on you. You are going to have to think for yourself. Try to think positively—about what is really good for you, for your partner, and for your relationship—instead of thinking up outer limits of morality. And if you are really close to your partner, you had better discuss it together, before you're involved—not after.

Can petting be harmful?

Q: My boyfriend and I have been going together for six months. We believe that the Lord brought us together. I'm fifteen and he is seventeen. We get along amazingly well and never fight or argue. We try to help each other and work out our problems. We definitely are in love. If our feelings continue in the future, we would love to be married.

We both understand that the intimacy of sex should be experienced only after the commitment of marriage. We know that to start having sex now would be a mistake as well as a sin. But what about "petting" or "touching"? Sometimes our emotions are so strong, it seems like the right thing to do.

We are not sure if it, too, is a sin. It's hard to understand why it feels so beautiful if it isn't right. It makes us feel so close that it's totally amazing. If "touching" or "petting" is a sin in the sight of God, we should stop and wait until we marry, if we do. But how do we know what we should be doing? Please help us, we are both so confused.

A: Let's start with a definition. By "petting" people may mean one or more actions in a range of different actions:

1. hugging so that your hands caress your partner's back and sides
2. touching breasts and groin through clothing
3. touching breasts and groin under the clothing
4. lying down together or one on top of the other
5. touching sexual organs
6. touching sexual organs in order to reach orgasm

People in biblical times probably would have assumed that any activity on my list is a preliminary to sexual intercourse—as, indeed, all of them are within marriage. The question is: Should a couple enjoy some of these preliminaries of lovemaking while "stopping short" of making love? As you point out, the preliminaries feel good and feel loving when two people care for each other. Yet they don't go "all the way," don't do what may lead to pregnancies, herpes, AIDS, etc. Is only sexual intercourse off limits for unmarried people? Or is there some other line short of intercourse where we ought to stop?

I think there is. The Bible doesn't guide us directly, and it's possible for different Christians to make up their minds in different ways. Whether you agree or disagree with my conclusions, I hope you'll arrive at some definite standards of your own. You've been working backwards—trying something out, then considering whether it's right or not. That's a recipe for rationalization. It's better to decide what you believe is right in advance and then stick to it.

I rule out two extremes from the beginning. On the one hand, I disagree with those Christians who think that couples should treat each other as "brother and sister" until they are married. That's an imaginary world, and we should live in the real world. People of the opposite sex feel romantically attracted to each other and have no reason to be embarrassed by that fact. It's good, because God made us that way. I believe that communicating the attraction to each other is okay, if it is done with caution and genuine concern to protect each other from harm. When people try to pretend the feelings aren't there, they often end up with phony relationships.

On the other hand, I disagree with those who make virginity a technicality—a question of one organ penetrating another. They say that so long as two people don't have actual sexual intercourse they are all right. I say that God's concern for virginity is not a matter of anatomy but of privacy. He wants people to reserve some "private parts" for their married partner alone. Only in marriage ought two people to be naked and unashamed, as Adam and Eve were. When two people touch each other's sexual organs, I believe they are doing what is appropriate for married people alone. Therefore, 5 and 6 on my list are out of bounds.

I would, additionally, put 2, 3, and 4 out of bounds. They're not so intimate as touching sexual organs. Yet I think they are more harmful than helpful to a relationship like yours. Here are my reasons for thinking so:

1. *They cause frustration.* They are natural preliminaries to sexual intercourse, and when you do them, you want to go on. When you make yourself stop short instead, you'll feel frustration. Usually guys feel this frustration more directly and immediately than girls do. The farther you go, the harder stopping becomes. I have yet to hear that frustration is helpful to a relationship. Often it blocks good communication by dominating your time together.

2. *Petting feels good, but it will not continue to feel as good as it does at first.* Gradually it will become more frustrating than fulfilling. It's a general rule of the body. Holding hands

gives a tremendous thrill the first time, but eventually it just gives sweat. Kissing has atomic power early on, but becomes quite routine later. The same is true of all forms of petting. After a while, they don't thrill the way they did. The body wants to go on and won't settle down at any level short of going all the way. Therefore, any beautiful feelings tend to be short-term, and you don't need short-term good feelings. You want whatever builds a good relationship long-term.

3. *Touching does lead to other things.* It doesn't have to, but it is hard to stop and keep stopping over months and years together. When you're fifteen and talking about marriage, you're looking at the possibility of three to seven years of stopping. It's a long time to wait. You're a great deal more likely to survive if you set limits you can easily live with— rather than stimulating "beautiful feelings" so you will constantly think of going farther.

4. *These areas of the body are private.* They are not so private as the sexual organs, but I think they represent a degree of intimacy that is out of place between two people who are just going together.

Where do you draw the line, then? That's probably different for different cultures. Conservative Muslims are convinced that even *seeing* each other is too provocative. They would look on kissing as completely decadent. In our culture, I think kissing and hugging are fine, especially if the couple does not do it for too long at a time. (If you kiss for more than ten minutes at a time, you're either looking for trouble, or you're trying to wear out your lips. A fifteen-minute kiss does not communicate more love and tenderness than a two-minute kiss. It just communicates more desire.) As part of that, I'd allow caressing the back and sides. But I'd keep my hands off any private areas of the body.

And let's be clear: kissing and hugging do bring out beautiful, romantic feelings. They are not "second-rate" in any way. In some ways they make a far warmer, more personable demonstration of love than petting does, for they are not so charged with urgent sexual desires.

One more question, which I am sure you will want to

ask: How do we stop doing whatever we've enjoyed doing so much? I know it is not easy to do. Most people think they've got their sexuality well under control until they try quitting something they've become accustomed to doing. Then they discover the untamed power of sex as an element of life we humans barely control, if at all.

So far as I know, the only effective way to stop is to start over. Don't try to back up your physical intimacy just one notch. Start as though you've only just met, and keep it very formal physically—with no involvement at all. This will feel just rotten. But you need to get your body back to the point where it finds holding hands an incredible privilege—which, indeed, it is.

Is there really any harm in making out?

Q: My problem is a problem many teens face. At the age of seventeen, people find it hard to make decisions on the subject of sex. How far should we go? Is there really any limit? Is making out a step away from God? These are just a few questions asked by many, I'm sure. Parents often say sex is a no-no until marriage, but they never say anything about what comes before sex and marriage. Is there really any harm in making out and feeling out? Please explain some answers. I'm quite confused.

A: The Bible doesn't give us any specific guidance on modern dating and courtship. It does give these very broad principles: Sex is for marriage, and lust is wrong. The Bible never defines lust exactly, but the basic idea is clear: we're to be pure in our attitudes as well as our actions.

Some people think making out is incompatible with this.

They think it's for married people only. I don't. Touching and kissing do raise lots of problems, but I don't believe they're wrong in themselves.

But making out can certainly bring problems. Many couples who had very pure intentions to keep sex for marriage end up saying, "We couldn't stop. And we didn't want to stop!" If you never get started, you don't have that problem.

A second problem is that touching and kissing often make a relationship seem much more significant than it really is. In reality, the two of you may have very little in common, but sexual excitement carries you away, and you feel in love. Sooner or later this wears off, and you are left with a variety of other feelings: guilt, regret, anger, disappointment. People have enough bad experiences at romance without creating conditions that encourage disappointment.

A third problem is that kissing and touching often preoccupy relationships. Most people aren't poets or great orators who can express their feelings and their ideas very well. Rather than try, many people use a great deal of precious time speaking body language. This problem can be intensified for couples who don't want to go all the way. You still crave a certain feeling, a certain thrill. But your body is built in such a way that wherever you draw the line short of intercourse, whether holding hands or no holds barred, that thrill wears off. You keep trying harder to make it reappear, and it won't, except for very short periods of time. If you're not careful, your whole relationship begins to circle around the time when you try to get that feeling again. Touching and feeling do not nourish a relationship very well, though. Talking does. A great many relationships with great potential never got anywhere because the two people gave up talking for touching.

A fourth and final problem is that touching and kissing can create shame. I wish I had a dollar for every letter I've received from someone in agony, months or years later, from the shame created by some quick pleasure. Sex, of course, has the greatest potential for this, but, short of that, going "too far" creates plenty of it too.

We Christians should not be playing body squeeze just to feel pleasing sensations run up and down our bodies. We could do that with somebody we met on the street. No, if we touch someone, we should do it to show our love and excitement in who that person is.

My first principle, then, is that you have no reason to touch or kiss someone the first time you go out together. Nor, probably, the second and third times either. I realize that social convention demands that a couple kiss (if not more) on the first date. If you mean "peck," I have no objections. That kind of kiss may be just a social greeting. But the kind of kiss you get wet with means more. If it doesn't, it should. So I believe that kissing and touching should not enter a relationship until you have developed a genuine, deep appreciation for each other's personality. That takes time.

My second principle is that the language of touch has no dictionary, and so terms must be defined. A kiss may mean next to nothing to one person and a great deal to someone else. You cannot be sure of your partner's feelings without talking it out, and talking with a very sensitive ear, listening for subtle nuances in the other's words. You want to agree together, beforehand, what kind of activity expresses best the kind of love you feel for each other. I wouldn't recommend that you revise your agreements in mid-date, either; you may not be altogether rational. As you grow more deeply in love, you may want to "say" more with your touch. What's appropriate for an engaged couple is not the same as for a couple who have been going out for a month.

There's a point to watch carefully here. Of the many relationships you form in your life, all but one will certainly break down. Usually it takes one or both of you some time to realize that your relationship isn't going anywhere, and in that interim period you will be tempted to hype your feelings by increased application of the hands and mouth. This will not affect the root cause of frustration, but it can prolong the agony of your parting and create shame that will last long after your relationship is otherwise forgotten. If you're in doubt about your future together, lay off. You need more time to talk, anyway, not touch.

My third principle is perhaps the most important of all: the principle of diminishing returns. To a point, the farther you go, the more love you express. But another corresponding principle cancels these gains out. The farther you go, the more frustrating it is to stop. You end an evening, not purring with delight, but frustrated by pent-up desire. You feel angry without reason. You haven't expressed love at all in such a condition.

This means that you reach a point of diminishing returns. By going farther, you may theoretically express more love. But the greater frustration you create outweighs it. No matter how much you love each other, you should stop before you reach that point. The frustration will not only hurt your relationship, but it will also put you into the temptation to go much farther.

There are three aspects to this "line of diminishing returns." The first is the precise activity you engage in. This is what everybody thinks of: How should I kiss? What should I touch? As I said, the language varies with various people. Holding hands may be too frustrating for some. I don't want to arouse guilt or raise an artificial barrier. I will offer this generality, though: I have neither experienced nor known of a situation where doing more than kissing and hugging increased the sense of love in the long run. Touching bare skin, breasts, etc., nearly always seems to lead to intense sexual frustration. So I would say, leave it at kissing and hugging. I don't think it can do you any harm to stop there, and it could save you quite a bit of harm. I am sure you won't miss anything. The sexual excitement in touching a forbidden part is exactly that of holding hands—for the first time only. After that the pleasure diminishes and the frustration increases.

The second aspect of a "line" is time. Few people talk about this, but there is certainly a difference between doing something briefly and keeping it up for two and a half hours. I wish somebody had warned me about this when I was seventeen. You need to decide not just what activity you'll engage in, but for how long. The temptation is to continue until all pleasure is gone, until you feel as though you're making out with a football.

The third aspect of a "line" is sexual arousal. A time comes when love stops mattering and sexual desire takes over. There's nothing wrong with it. It's just a feeling and a perfectly good one. But I take it as a sign that you should quit. Stand up and walk around for a while until you calm down. Go take a stroll in the park or visit your local shopping mall. It is far easier to do that when you first notice the desire than later on. It takes discipline to stop there, but experience will tell you that what occurs after that point is mainly frustration.

I often hear from people who are involved in petting (or sex), and who say that they don't feel guilty or even frustrated; they just feel closer to that person than ever. They say their relationship has improved. I'm sure they're telling the truth, so far as they can see it. In the short term, the wonderfully intimate feelings brought by sexual touching can draw people closer together. At least they feel closer.

But I also hear from people months or years later. Then they rarely—I would say almost never—look on petting as having been helpful. They see how the closeness it brought was superficial. They see how sex slowly came to dominate their relationship. These people struggle to forget, and they wonder just how much of what they experienced will have to be explained to a future partner. Petting doesn't really help a relationship. It harms it.

What if we can't agree on how far to go?

Q: My girlfriend and I have been going together for quite some time now. We are very much a part of each other's life. We love each other more than anyone else in the world. Our love is growing so fast we need new ways to show it. We kiss and hold each other close, but to me that does not show my love enough. We talked before about petting and things of that sort. I have no intention of going "all the way." She said she didn't know if petting was really right or if God wanted her to do such things. I tried to find things in the Bible that said it was wrong, but I couldn't find any. My girlfriend then said she would know it was right when something told her it was. Until then, she didn't want to. But I love her so dearly that I need a new way of showing it. What can I do?

A: You can start by cutting out the pressure on your girlfriend. That would be a very practical way of showing her you love and respect her. Even if petting were a good way to show love, it wouldn't be if your girlfriend were pushed into it. It would be like expressing love by sending flowers to a girl who's allergic to them.

Besides, there are other ways to express love. You don't have to say things physically; in fact, that may be the poorest way. By talking together, by doing things together, and by playing and working together you express a kind of love that is more meaningful. It may not *feel* more meaningful, but in the long run it will prove to be so. Too many love affairs go wrong because the physical side takes over.

Is petting wrong when you're engaged?

Q: My fiancée and I are both Christians. Both she and I want to serve and live for the Lord with all our might! But we have one problem: SEX! I need to know how far is going "too far."

We haven't had sexual intercourse, and won't until we're

married. But we have petted very heavily. Out of love for each other we want to give ourselves physically as well as spiritually and mentally. We don't see making out as a "dirty" act because we are in love and sex seems a clean feeling. We soon will be married and then sex will be a part of our daily lives.

But we still sometimes feel guilty. I can't turn off my desires, and neither can my fiancée, but we want to do what's right. When you are engaged, is petting wrong? Does the Bible say anything about this?

A: The Bible is silent on this question, which probably didn't come up very often in a culture where there was very little contact between men and women before marriage—even when they were engaged.

Let me offer my opinion: I don't think petting before marriage is a good idea, regardless of how much you love each other or how soon you'll be married. I'll tell you why.

Petting isn't one thing: it covers many actions, starting with fondling breasts or genital areas, and going on in intensity all the way to climax. Our bodies are built in such a way that one message comes through all along the continuum: Farther. Go farther. If you're going to listen to God, you can't obey that voice until you're married; you have to draw a line somewhere and say, "We must stop here."

That's frustrating. It might be nice if petting could be simply an expression of love, but it doesn't work that way. It's a physical expression of love that leads naturally on to something greater. To stop that natural process in the middle usually leaves you feeling overheated and incomplete. I can't see creating frustration as a positive expression of love in any relationship, at any time.

The fact that you're engaged changes some things. If you do in fact marry (though not all engaged couples make it to the church), your premarital experiences won't ever have to be "confessed" to someone else. Also, your commitment to marriage does change the intimacy of your relationship. For example, it's appropriate for engaged couples to talk about very personal matters that they would never discuss with anyone else, such as financial matters and sexual matters.

But the frustration brought on by petting and stopping doesn't change. Even the day before your wedding it won't change. I can't see any good in it. And wouldn't you feel better on your wedding day if you hadn't put yourself through it?

The more time and energy you put into making out, the less time you'll spend getting to know each other. That's the whole point of your engagement, isn't it? You want time to get to know each other deeply. Petting interferes with that. Believe me, after you're married you are going to need all the mutual understanding you can possibly build before the wedding day. You'll have plenty of time and much better circumstances to get to know each other sexually after marriage; but this time of exploring each other's personality is something precious you will never have again. Who loves talking together more than the starry-eyed couple? Who else can enjoy such simple (and ordinarily irritating) things as shopping together? Who gives gifts more than those newly in love? It is a shame that often, after the wedding, these expressions of love stop. Before the wedding, make the most of them. They express love, and they build a basis for further love, because they lead to greater understanding—something that petting will never do.

Finally, guilt, whether justified or not, isn't good for your relationship. Petting can lead to guilt feelings, as it has for you. Something about exposing yourself that far without total commitment often leaves you feeling naked, even indecent. Those feelings hurt you and your relationship. Sex doesn't deserve to be accompanied by guilt—it's worth more than that.

Isn't it better to pet than to make love?

Q: I love my boyfriend, and we both feel that sex is wrong until marriage. But we both get that temptation, and we fight it off with heavy petting. Looking at all my friends who have had sex, we see how it leads to abortions, miscarriages, and premature marriages. I can't say I feel guilty about heavy petting. I feel almost proud that my boyfriend and I have a limit and that we don't have to face those problems.

I'm not saying our relationship is based on heavy petting. We have a very open and understanding relationship. But at times we need each other physically. I really feel he is the one for me and that God wants us together. Are we wrong for what we are doing and for the way we feel?

A: If I understand you correctly, by heavy petting you mean touching each other to the point of orgasm. You see it as a sexual release that keeps you from having intercourse and getting pregnant. You don't want to be pushed into marriage or abortion or anything else by the unavoidable consequences of pregnancy.

So far as I can see, however, God's opposition to premarital sex has little or nothing to do with the fear of pregnancy. If he were concerned about that, proper birth control would make premarital sex right in his eyes. Yet in all that the Bible says about sex, it never says one warning word about pregnancy. My guess is that God knows of no such thing as an "unwanted child." Any child is good to him; pregnancy itself is not a bad thing but a good thing.

God's concern seems to be people and their relationships. He sees sex as the ultimate intimacy, capable of expressing the love of men and women, capable also of destroying and distorting their love. Many people in our time think of sex as something like Play-Doh—pretty, flexible stuff that you can play with and enjoy any way you like as long as you don't grind it into the carpet. The biblical view is more like this: Sex is dynamite, capable of moving mountains, but also capable of tearing you apart. You don't play with dynamite, you use it very carefully—and in just the right spot.

The "right spot" is marriage. There two people who have committed themselves in love to each other can, in complete and utter shamelessness, give their bodies to each other. They never have to leave each other and go home. They don't have to worry about pregnancy or anything else. They can be secure, knowing that their commitment is forever. Neither person is going to dump the other. And they share the daily, gritty responsibilities of life together—finances, children, taking out the garbage. These responsibilities are not all pleasant, but they help keep a couple growing in love. Married people have to work out so many things that they grow to know each other better—and thus can love each other better. In such circumstances, it is perfectly natural for them to go "all the way." Their growing understanding of each other feeds their love.

You're not there yet. I hope you get there, if you're right for each other. But until you arrive there, the naked openness of sex would be a mistake.

While heavy petting is not the same as intercourse, it does share many of the same psychological characteristics: no parts kept private, nothing held back. The same reasons that premarital sex is a problem are also valid for heavy petting. It is intimacy meant for a climate of total involvement and total commitment.

I know quite well the physical need you feel for each other. It is strong. But there are other ways to deal with it. It is not just a biological urge you need to satisfy occasionally, like the need to eat. It is also the tremendously creative urge of love. If you turn the energy into other channels, being as creative as you can to express your love in nonsexual ways, it will have the effect of drawing you toward each other.

Try running together, writing poems, singing, giving

simple gifts. No, you won't be totally satisfied. But that's okay. The deeply exciting, unsatisfied attraction you have for each other is the peculiar joy of courtship. It's like the days before Christmas. You're waiting to open the presents. You're preparing.

That never gets old. But sexual intercourse, or heavy petting, will. People who aren't married have very limited raw material to feed their love. They don't face problems together. They see each other only on social occasions. Sex nearly always gets old to them. So does the relationship. Most relationships break apart—even between people who felt very strongly that they belonged together. But if they've been sexually intimate, they break apart with much deeper wounds and much thicker scar tissue than they would otherwise suffer.

That's what I fear for you. I'm glad you haven't become pregnant. You have done better than your friends. But you aren't doing as well as you could. I fear that you will not keep growing closer together and that when boredom sets in, you will split, full of memories of intimacy that came too easily, memories that won't go away.

But petting has brought us closer to each other!

Q: Right from the beginning of our relationship, three months ago, I let David know my standards. I had never let a guy touch me; I wanted to save it all for my future husband. David agreed to everything. He was pretty experienced and I was scared at first that he'd drop me if I wouldn't let him do anything. But I was going to stick to my standards even if it meant losing him.

As time went on, I found that David wasn't like that at all. He didn't do anything I didn't want him to. I grew to really love him, and vice-versa. The problem is this: I started to really want him to touch me and show me his love. So one night, when he tried something, I didn't stop him. I encouraged him, and since then we've been doing a lot of light petting. Dave was worried that I'd regret it and feel guilty, so he volunteered to quit, but I told him it was all right.

Our relationship is strong and grows better every day. The physical part is simply to show our love. Since we began light petting, David has told me that he wants to make love to me, but he respects the way I feel. We talk about it a lot, and I've clipped out articles from your column and we've discussed them.

I definitely will wait for marriage, but the trouble is that Dave and I are coming close to heavy petting. I know this is only a short step away from making love, and I'm afraid I couldn't say no. David and I would stop our physical relationship if we thought it was hurting us or becoming the most important thing. But it's truly just our way of showing each other the love we feel for the other, and it's brought us closer.

I've always heard it's wrong, but now that I think about it, I don't know why. I'd appreciate your comments.

A: The age-old question is, "How far can I go?" That is the wrong question. The question should be, "How far should I go? What is good for me and my partner, for our relationship?"

One good thing about petting: it can make you feel good, and closer to each other. I would have to question your statement that it brings you closer together. Feeling closer and actually being closer are two different things. I doubt that any kind of kiss or caress makes a couple closer. Very often it has the opposite effect, preoccupying them so that they can't talk and do other things together nearly so much. Kisses and caresses express love and bring out good feelings; they don't create love.

But there is nothing wrong with expressing love, and there's quite a bit of good in feeling close to each other. So why not express love in petting? There is only one "why not" I know of, and that is simply that petting is emotionally and sexually very potent. It may be an innocent expression of love at the beginning, but it has a definite tendency to grow, to push for further and further intimacy and to become an end in itself.

Of course, as you found out, kissing is like that too. (That's one reason why hours of kissing is a bad idea.) But petting has a great deal more emotional impact than kissing. Once you begin to go under some clothes, it is easier to get rid of all of them. You can easily become two bodies lusting for each other, rather than two people loving and enjoying each other.

That is why, if I were you, I would cut out petting. When you try to stop, I think you will find that it has more of a hold on you than you think. Petting is not such an innocent expression of love as it seems: it has a power all its own, and it definitely does not want you to go back to the smaller fun of only kissing. It has begun, you say, as a way of expressing love. Experience shows that it can become a way of destroying love, too.

If my motive is love, how can petting be wrong in God's eyes?

Q: I am a college student who has always considered petting to be wrong. Recently I talked to a Christian friend who has different convictions. I found myself faced with some difficult questions. I would like your opinion on them.

I realize that God judges our motives and our hearts. Is it possible to pet purely out of love, with no wrong motives, and if so, does this make petting (with pure motives) acceptable in God's sight?

A: Thanks for writing. Your question is good. It applies not only to petting but to all kinds of behavior. People ask the same question when they say, "What's wrong with premarital sex when we love each other?" or even, "Is it a sin to lie to someone if you really mean well?" The presupposition is that God cares mainly about our motives. Carried to a logical extreme, this means that it doesn't really matter what you do, so long as you think loving thoughts while you do it. The Christian life thus becomes a mental exercise, and righteousness a psychological phenomenon.

This idea came into existence, I suppose, because Jesus taught that God cares about your inner self. For example, Jesus taught that it is not enough to avoid being a murderer; you must also not hate. But Jesus never taught that what you feel like inside is all that matters. He taught that lust is as bad as adultery, but he never suggested that adultery is all right if the two people love each other.

The Bible's position is that some actions are, in themselves, wrong. (That's what the Ten Commandments are all about.) But the Bible goes even further. God's rules are meant to penetrate beneath the action, way down into your deepest attitudes.

Petting is a difficult case, because though the Bible sets a definite boundary (sex outside of marriage is wrong), it doesn't give specific guidelines about the physical expressions that lead up to sex. I believe that petting is a mistake. It leads to frustration, it takes up time, it tempts you to go farther—and I can't see any really positive benefits. Petting feels good for a time, but the frustration that results feels worse. You may disagree with my analysis, but make sure of this: If petting is wrong, it is wrong no matter what cloud of romantic love you cover it with. What you think does matter to God, but so does what you do.

Are you still a virgin if you've had oral sex?

Q: I have a very strong difference of opinion with one of my male friends. I have had oral sex. I don't think he knows for sure that I have, only that I have been involved in heavy petting. He claims that if you have had oral sex you are technically still a virgin, but that you are by no means innocent and that you are not a virgin morally.

I totally disagree. I am still innocent. And I still have very high morals. I think the fact that I am still a virgin underlines that. I'm definitely innocent as far as society is concerned. And I know that God has forgiven me for the mistakes that I have made. Yes, mistakes: I believe that oral sex is wrong and should not be performed before marriage. But unfortunately I had to learn that the hard way. It has taken me a long time, but I have learned to accept the fact that God has forgiven me and that my sin has been forgotten. Therefore I am still innocent!

It hurts me very much that my friend would not think of me as being innocent and that he would think that I am not a virgin. My roommate agrees that I am not innocent. Neither of them have made my mistake; compared to them maybe I'm not innocent. But if I'm not innocent before them, then how can I be innocent before God?

It makes it so hard for me to get over my past when my two closest friends are so perfect when it comes to sex. I guess what I'm asking is, can you have oral sex and still be innocent before God? Am I only half a virgin?

A: Maybe it's just a difference of terminology, but I wouldn't have called you innocent even before you had oral sex. I don't think anybody is innocent, including your roommate and your male friend. The best any of us can be is forgiven—and that is very good indeed.

God has no problems with you, none whatsoever. Neither should your friends. There's no point in tallying the badness of past sins. They're all bad, bad enough to kill us. Romans 3:10–12 sums it up this way: "There is no one righteous, not even one; there is no one who understands, no one who seeks God. All have turned away, they have together become worthless." But that isn't the end of the story. For Romans goes on to show how the good news of Jesus saves us and cleanses us, leading to these good words: "There is now no condemnation for those who are in Christ Jesus" (8:1). You don't need to claim you're innocent. Claim that you are forgiven and that you're living in Jesus.

5. *Why Wait?*

Does God say to wait—and if so, why?

Q: I've been dating the same guy for almost eight months now. We've struggled with physical temptations. Ever since I was old enough to know what sex is, I've been told to avoid it because it's "naughty." But I've never been told straight out why, except for the possibility of pregnancy. Is it not true that in Bible days people didn't go through all the things needed to get married these days? Didn't they simply love each other enough to be committed, and live together as "married"? They were also considered adults at a much younger age.

If two people are really committed to each other, really care for each other, and understand the possible results of their intimacy, why is it wrong for them to make love?

A: I'm glad you've raised these questions. Too often people don't ask them out loud. I've had many, many people tell me, "I was raised to think that marriage was the right place for sex, and I intended to wait." But when they fell in love, and felt the tremendous physical urge to be close to someone else, their plan went out of the window. They just hadn't thought deeply enough about their reasons for waiting.

Our grandparents may have stayed out of trouble purely because "nice people don't do that kind of thing." But today nice people do. The Christian view of sex has become a minority position in America. It will have to be explained, not assumed. That's what I'd like to try to do.

I can't answer "what's wrong" without first answering "what's right." Sex outside of marriage isn't bad because it's "naughty," but because it gets in the way of something far better.

The Bible makes perfectly clear that God is not against sex. He invented it. He thought it was great. The Bible says that the first man and the first woman, introduced to each other by God himself, "were both naked, and they felt no shame" (Genesis 2:25). That's the way God meant it to be.

It isn't as though God couldn't have made procreation happen any other way. We might grow from cuttings, the way some plants do. That would be efficient—and boring. I could plant my fingernail clippings, and nine months later, up would come babies. God preferred to arrange it so that babies were made through an intimate, ecstatic embrace. Having invented sex, he clearly intends people to enjoy it.

But sex is not at the top of all God's gifts. *He had even better things in mind.* God meant sex to go with love—with love that never ends. Sex gives its greatest joy in a relationship of love that lasts forever. That's what God wants you to experience. That's why God is against premarital sex.

The love that goes with premarital sex usually doesn't last forever. Sometimes it doesn't last a week. God is delighted when two people who love each other deeply have sex. What he can't stand is when people who are bonded together by that kind of intimacy break apart. Feelings aren't enough to hold them together. We need the marriage commitment to strengthen our love.

You are correct in saying that people in the Bible didn't necessarily go through elaborate marriage ceremonies. The story of Isaac and Rebekah in Genesis 24 may be typical. Rebekah and her family agreed to her marriage to Isaac, and so she moved into his tent. There was no church, no ceremony, no vows that we know of.

This system worked—and still works in some parts of the world—because people had a very close-knit family structure with a very clear understanding of what was expected of each individual. Everybody knew the commitment that was involved when a man and a woman moved into a home together. The commitment wasn't any less: they just didn't need a ceremony to show it.

In today's world we use a legal and religious ceremony to mark a new commitment. We don't live in tight-knit extended families. We need the ceremony.

At any rate, the ceremony isn't really the issue. Most people who are ready to commit their lives to each other are quite happy to throw a big party for all their family and friends. They feel delighted to participate in a solemn religious ceremony where they spell out their vows.

I don't think you're really questioning the marriage ceremony. You're questioning whether it's necessary to put off sex until you are ready to make such a total commitment. Wouldn't it be enough to merely *feel* committed?

But the Bible, from beginning to end, asks for solid commitment *at the beginning* from those who want to sleep together. The rule is simple: no commitment, no sex.

And the Bible doesn't recognize a halfway, "maybe" commitment. You ask whether sex would be okay between two people who are "really committed to each other." Committed for what? Committed for "as long as we both shall love"? Committed until you don't feel committed any more? Committed until you fall out of love?

As Jesus put it, "What God has joined together, let man not separate" (Matthew 19:6). If you're not ready to commit yourself for a lifetime of loving, don't get "joined" in sexual intercourse.

Why not? Not simply because premarital sex is "naughty," but because sex before marriage—sex without complete commitment—is like dessert before the meal. It can spoil your appetite for really healthy food. People who have sex without commitment often never get to the commitment. People who try sex without marriage find lasting, loving relationships hard to create.

That's what's happening in our society. Look around you. Don't you think there is some correlation between sexual freedom and broken families?

It's been well documented that people who live together

before marriage are considerably less likely to create a lasting marriage.

The Bible says that when you go to bed, something happens to the two of you, something that changes you at the deepest level. You are bound together body and soul. You can't just painlessly back away from the relationship any more than you can separate two pieces of paper that have been glued together. You can tear the two pieces apart, but not without leaving pieces of one stuck forever to the other. Paul talks about that in 1 Corinthians 6:12–20.

Our world is full of hurting people who have been glued to a dozen different people. They've become hard with glue and tattered with pieces of ex-lovers. They keep on gluing themselves to new partners, hoping to make up for the damage already done. But they become less and less capable of bonding to someone for life.

Don't start that process. Sex is an incredible gift in the right context. In the wrong context it's an incredible source of heartbreak and lifebreak. You don't want to join two lives together unless you are as sure as is humanly possible they will never be torn apart again. That means marriage—full-hearted, committed marriage.

Don't kid yourself into thinking that *feelings*, however strong, are a substitute.

Does the Bible really say premarital sex is wrong?

Q: Column after column, you stress that premarital sex is wrong and give biblical verses such as Matthew 15:19; 1 Corinthians 6:9–10; or Colossians 3:5–6 supporting *your* opinion. However, these biblical verses never state that premarital sex is wrong, they just say stay away from sexual sin. How are we supposed to know what is sexual sin and what is not? With all the hate and war in this world, making love does not seem sinful.

A: Good question. Since the Bible was put together almost 2,000 years ago and was written in Hebrew, Aramaic, and Greek, the advice it gives isn't always easy to translate directly into modern American English. That's particularly true in this question of premarital sex.

The immediate problem, which you've caught, is translation. You (and I) would prefer it if the Bible said flat out, "No premarital sex allowed." But there isn't any New Testament Greek term for "premarital sex." The word the Bible uses, a word that is translated "sexual immorality" or "sexual sin" (or "fornication" in the older translations), is *porneia*. Not all scholars agree on how *porneia* should be translated, but the most common belief is that it's a broad word for sexual immorality, having a specific meaning only in specific contexts. "Casual sex" or "sexual immorality" might be a modern way to put it.

At first glance, it looks as though the word *porneia* is so general it doesn't help at all. As you put it, how are we supposed to know what is sexual sin and what is not? But if you look carefully at the whole Bible's teaching about sex, the answer becomes a lot clearer. The New Testament presents only one proper place for sexual intercourse: within marriage.

In those days when virginity for women was considered valuable, there wasn't anything like dating or going steady. People married young. Most people old enough to be interested in sex were already married. If someone went looking for sex outside of marriage, his main options were prostitution or adultery. But both of these are labeled very clearly as wrong in the Bible.

Adultery is wrong (Exodus 20:14). Casual sex with prostitutes is wrong (1 Corinthians 6:15–17). Single people who lack sexual self-control are urged to marry, not to practice "safe sex" (7:2, 9) In all of the New Testament, you don't find a single hint of exceptions or loopholes. In fact,

Jesus says that even looking at another person with lust amounts to adultery (Matthew 5:27–30).

If the question is "Why doesn't the Bible say premarital sex is wrong?" the answer is "It does." It declares that marriage is the place for sex—and specifically states that the extramarital alternatives known in that day are wrong. For the first New Testament readers the broad word *porneia* was evidently clear enough. They knew what it meant, just as our grandparents understood what "sexual immorality" meant. They understood that it meant all sex outside of marriage.

The real question isn't what the Bible says about premarital sex, but whether today is different. People wait a long time to marry today. While they are waiting, they go out on dates. In this new situation, would it be wrong for two people who really love each other but aren't ready for the commitment of marriage to make love? Maybe the people who wrote the Bible never thought of that. Personally I doubt that they did, any more than they imagined teenagers driving around on Saturday nights. However, I can't see any reason to imagine that they would have felt more favorable about sex outside of marriage in our situation than they thought about it in theirs.

What makes premarital sex in our situation different from what it was in those days? One answer people give is birth control. In those days, sex meant babies, and there was no way to prevent conception. Maybe now that two people with a pill can have sex "without consequences," sex has become harmless (so long as the two people love each other).

But this difference doesn't hold up. First, we've seen ample evidence that birth control hasn't eliminated unwanted pregnancies. One and a half million abortions and even more children born out of wedlock in the U.S. each year would suggest that sex and pregnancy go together as much as ever.

Even if they didn't go together, I don't see any reason to believe it would change the Bible's position. We view pregnancy as a big problem, but it evidently wasn't a problem in biblical societies. There's not one single word in the Bible about babies being "unwanted." The Bible's concern with premarital sex isn't babies, but what happens spiritually between two people who have sex. (1 Corinthians 6:12–20 and 1 Thessalonians 4:3–8 take this up in the most detail.) Those spiritual realities aren't changed by birth control.

Other people say that what makes premarital sex different in our time is love. They point out that in New Testament days sex outside of marriage meant either cheating on a marriage (adultery) or some kind of sex for money (prostitution). Today two people may sleep together because they feel powerfully swept up in love. Isn't that different? Doesn't love make it right?

It is different, but I can't see why that difference would have made any difference to the biblical writers. When Paul urges married people to develop a loving relationship (Ephesians 5:25–33), it's very obvious that he's not talking about powerful, temporary emotions, but commitment to serve and care for each other, regardless of what comes. He's talking about the kind of love God shows us, which doesn't run out tomorrow—or ever. That's true love. It's not feelings, it's commitment. Within it, sex becomes lovely and holy. Outside it, sex often turns out to be ugly and harmful—and how you felt when you first went to bed together doesn't make much difference in that.

One more point: You write, "With all the hate and war in the world, making love does not seem sinful." I guess that takes us back to one of your earlier questions: How are we supposed to know when something is immoral and when it isn't?

One fact the Bible shouts loud and clear is that, by ourselves, we're not very good judges. We tend to justify whatever we do. Take a look at all that "hate and war" you mention and see whether you can find anybody who really accepts blame. The Arabs blame the Israelis, the Israelis blame the Arabs; the Catholics blame the Protestants, the Protestants blame the Catholics—and nobody ever accepts the fact that he himself is responsible. That's why God's word is so valuable. It tells us, independent of our own emotions and self-justification, how to judge a situation. We desperately need that aid.

Making love may seem rather innocent, compared to some things that go on. But that doesn't make it right. Shoplifting at the mall may seem rather innocent compared to armed robbery, but that's a weak justification for shoplifting. If you play the comparison game, you can make everything short of the Holocaust seem innocent.

I could make a good argument that premarital sex is as destructive as any force in our society today. All those abortions, all those unwanted children (who contribute tremendously to poverty and thus to crime, addiction, and the horrible cycle of people stuck in the ghetto), the more widespread pattern of sexual unfaithfulness and divorce and broken homes, and the plague of AIDS and other sexually transmitted diseases—don't those have anything to do with "innocent" premarital sex? It doesn't seem farfetched at all to believe that the Bible's warnings against sexual immorality are just as relevant today as ever, and it becomes clear that sex is meant for marriage—and nowhere else.

What if no one is hurt by premarital sex—is it still wrong?

Q: I'm eighteen. I have dated frequently since I was fifteen. Most of my dates are non-Christians, though I consider myself a Christian. I believe in Christ, and he is an important part of my life.

Until lately my dates and I always discussed sex. I believed sex was meant for marriage, and outside of that it would only hurt the relationship. I have never had a guy hassle me on my limits. I don't think I was being unrealistic or prudish about it.

A few weeks ago, my boyfriend and I doubled with

another couple. I thought I knew the girl fairly well. She appears to have a good relationship with Christ. She is very active in her church and frequently brings friends there. She reads your magazine and passes it on to non-Christians. But she surprised me by getting drunk and jumping into bed with her date.

That night was the first time my boyfriend ever contested my limit. If my very Christian girlfriend would do it, why shouldn't I? I could find no answer other than that it clashed with my beliefs and I didn't think we needed sex to show our love. He came back with, "If we love each other, how can sex hurt a relationship?" I had no answer.

We have been having sex now for weeks. We enjoy it and are careful. I'm confused. Why is it un-Christian to practice sex out of marriage if no one is hurt by it?

A: First of all, it's un-Christian because the Bible says it is. Sometimes "Christian" comes to mean whatever a person wants it to mean. But surely what is Christian ought to be defined by what the Bible says.

I suppose, however, that what you're really wanting to know is why the Bible defines sex outside of marriage as un-Christian. If it really stacked up as you say—if no one really were hurt by it—then the rule against it would be very hard to explain. But you don't have to look very far to see that you can be hurt by it—very, very badly.

Not that the hurt is always apparent immediately. For the present, sex may be simply an extremely enjoyable action—like kissing to the nth degree. But sex is a great deal more significant than that, as you'll find out in time—and as our sex-ravaged society is just beginning to discover through the pain of endless broken relationships and people reduced to bodies.

I'd define the significance of sex something like this: sex is an action between a man and a woman that binds them totally together—mentally, spiritually, physically. It is meant to express an exclusive, loving, total commitment to each other. It is meant to make them "family," forever.

I think that definition comes from the Bible. In discussing prostitution, 1 Corinthians 6:12–20 makes the strongest case; it says that even if you go to bed with a prostitute—by definition sex without commitment or love—you are "one flesh" with that person. You are powerfully, spiritually tied together. You can try as hard as you want to make it casual, but it's never casual. It's life and death.

You and your boyfriend are trying to have an enjoyable physical expression of your affection, believing that because you feel love for each other, no harm can come to either of you. But you've done something greater than you thought. It has all kinds of hidden effects that can hurt you.

It can hurt your relationship. By having sex you vastly, if subtly, change your relationship. Before you had sex, you were friends. Now you are totally naked with each other. Emotional needs and dependencies can arise slowly and almost invisibly, but they are very powerful. You'll find that the relationship is not nearly so casual as you had thought. Many couples discover that after a while things between them get weird.

Yet there's no commitment to hold you together and certainly very little time to work any problems out. You get together for a date and some sex, and then you split to your separate homes. Sexual intimacy is meant to be worked out between people who are full-time couples, married, sharing everything. It's meant for people who aren't giving a single thought to whether things are going to work out or not. They know they're committed to each other, for life. They have the time and security to solve problems together.

In having sex you've also canceled the mystery of sex between you. Most couples come back together repeatedly because they're intrigued and challenged by the unknowns of the other person. But you've now gone all the way. You feel, though it's not true, that there is nothing more to explore. You have a false sense of completeness. What you still need is to grow together; sex can prevent that by making you complacent.

The odds are extremely good that you and your boyfriend won't end up married for life. Very likely at some time in the future you'll split. The pain you experience from a broken sexual relationship is triple the pain you receive in a normal broken romance. You can't just walk away from someone you've had sex with. The memories stay with you—and you are never quite the same person again.

Premarital sex can hurt your *future* partners—including your marriage partner. You'll want to tell him about your past, and he may feel deeply hurt to know that you've been sexually intimate with others. But regardless of that, you'll carry to your next partner—including your future marriage partner—a set of habits: ways of thinking and acting that you'll tend to repeat and pass on. You'll bring memories of another person's body (very likely a whole series of bodies) and of sex with other people. You can't help comparing. Comparisons are not good for love. You can hurt the future someone you will least want to hurt.

You bring to your next partner not only memories but also a complete sharing of all the sexually transmitted diseases you or any of your past partners have been exposed to. If you've had five partners, and each of them had five partners, who each had five partners, you're sharing diseases with at least 125 people, to start. That can hurt you too—and hurt others.

The ideal is to enter marriage without any shadows from your past. The fact that you won't be able to do that means you have already hurt four people—yourself, your future husband, your boyfriend, and his future wife. It doesn't mean you've ruined your life. But you've certainly tarnished the best possibilities that married life has to offer. You may even be in danger of losing them.

What if both partners know the relationship is "just for now"? How can they be hurt?

Q: Not long ago you wrote that it would be very hard to explain why sex is wrong if no one were hurt by it. Perhaps I am an exception, but sex has never hurt me in the past seven years, and I can't believe that it ever could. I've never hurt another person by it either. Whenever you cite a Scripture that illustrates why sex is wrong, there is always reference made to a prostitute or a harlot. I do not consider myself to be either of these, and I find it hard to draw a definite conclusion based on these examples. I can't see why it is wrong to be "one flesh" with a person who means a great deal to me. It has only brought me closer to him and helped me to understand him better.

The reason I am asking your advice is that I want to be a good Christian but do not feel in my heart that sex, for me, is wrong. Marriage is out of the question because my career keeps me on the road most of the time and I am too committed to my work to give it up for any one man.

I am very careful that my partner's feelings correspond with my own. In this way, I am certain that I haven't hurt anyone because they all knew beforehand what to expect. You have also said that unless sex is a trivial thing to a person, it is hard to walk away from a broken relationship unhurt. I hope you can see that sex is far from trivial to me. Otherwise, I would not have bothered to write this letter. If you can find an example in the Bible that you feel applies to my situation, I will greatly appreciate it.

A: Sometimes you can hurt and be hurt without knowing it. I think that's the case with you.

In referring you to 1 Corinthians 6:15–20 I'm certainly

not suggesting that you are a prostitute. That passage does refer to prostitutes, but it offers principles about sex that apply to you and me.

The interesting point is why Paul says going to a prostitute is wrong. His reasons are not what you might expect—she's cheap, she's unclean, she's selling sex without love. Paul simply says that to have sex with her is to become "one flesh"—an intimate unity that makes two people one.

Sex, according to Paul, isn't just physical and emotional pleasure that you can enjoy and forget. It involves all of you, including your spiritual nature. In the right kind of relationship—in marriage—that's wonderful. In the wrong kind of relationship, it pollutes your life. Paul's objection to prostitution could just as easily serve as an objection to what you are doing.

You say you're not hurting anybody, because your partners know in advance that you're not planning on commitment. But since when does that guarantee no hurt? People may know in advance that jumping off a cliff involves a severe fall, but that doesn't keep them from breaking a leg when they land. When two people are bonded together in love, breaking apart *does* cause pain. Maybe you don't realize it now, but you probably have a lot more life to live. You don't know what you or your partners might come to regret when you look back on the uncommitted affairs you seem to thrive on.

But even more serious is the damage that you never learn to regret—damage that you don't even know you've done to yourself. You're leaving pieces of yourself with your partners. You're leaving them with memories they can never put out of their minds. You're making it impossible for them to later have sex with a wife and not compare her body, her sex, with yours. You're training them to treat sex as a promise that can easily be broken.

And these effects are not only happening to them. They're also happening to you.

The advice in Hebrews 13:4 applies here: "Marriage should be honored by all, and the marriage bed kept pure, for

God will judge the adulterer and all the sexually immoral." God wants the marriage bed kept pure. "Pure" means "unadulterated" or "containing one substance only." A pure marriage bed is one in which only one couple can be found— and no ghosts from the past. By playing with sex you're destroying that potential purity. That hurts.

We're really made for each other—doesn't that make it right to have sex?

Q: Just a few weeks ago Todd and I realized our need for each other. Both of us were involved in sexual relationships and desperately wanted to get out of them. In the back of our minds we knew they would never work out. Now both of us are trying to "get over" (I say that with much meaning) those relationships. Todd and I love each other very much. We have to lift each other up a lot, especially when our previous partners make us feel terrible (as they often do) for what we've done to them. It hurts us terribly to drop them, because of the pain they're feeling. It's really hard not to want to go back to them.

Todd and I feel like we were made for each other. He fits the description perfectly of what I had in mind and wanted for a husband, and I fit his for a wife. But there are so many complications to our relationship. First of all, there's an age difference; he's eighteen and I'm fifteen. My parents don't like me with someone who's so much older, although we don't think age matters right now. We need each other badly. My parents also don't understand why I need him so. They don't realize that I'm trying to break free from a bad relationship that will have bad effects on me for the rest of my life. I could never tell them about it; my dad is a minister and his shame and embarrassment would bring our family and his job to ruin.

Todd plans on waiting for me while I finish high school and he goes to college. Neither of us knows if it will last or not, but we are sure that the probability is very great. But Todd and I can't help but feel a lot of very strong physical desires for each other. So far we have only kissed, but the temptations are there, and from our very recent relationships it's hard not to want to express our love and need for each other by doing what was like a habit to us before. We keep thinking that if we do have sex it might become a habit again, but the way we feel for each other and understand each other lets us think it wouldn't be that way. We keep asking ourselves why we can't.

Your column has helped us a lot in understanding why we shouldn't, but it will be so hard to keep those present feelings about it. If we were meant to be together, we've got at least three years before we could get married, and even then I feel that I would be too young. Both of us having past experience in sex is going to make and has made it very hard not to start again, but we know that once we do start we won't be able to stop.

Todd is what I've been praying for: someone to help me get over my previous relationship. Todd and I really need some encouraging words to help us through our decision not to make love. We also need help in going through with our decision not to go back with our old partners. Having had sex in our previous relationships makes us feel like we have a gap in ours now. We feel we're missing the closeness we had with them. Why does it have to be so wrong for us to sleep together when we feel the way we do?

A: It depends a lot on what you mean by "so wrong." If you mean, will it make warts grow on you, or drive you crazy with guilt, or turn you into a slut, my answer is "Probably not." A great many people in America, faced with a situation like the one you describe, sleep together. To the casual observer they seem to be doing fine.

I'd define "wrong" differently, however. "Wrong" is "less than the best." God's rules aren't arbitrary, and they certainly aren't intended to keep us from enjoying ourselves. They are to protect us from harm and keep us on the path that is richest and best.

What is "best" for you and Todd? In the immediate future, it would feel "best" to have intercourse together. It would probably fill in that missing gap you feel. You know already the warmth that can come through sex.

But you also know how horrible it is to be in a sexual relationship that's going nowhere. You know the evil feelings that come when sex is just a habit between people who no longer love each other. That is certainly not "best."

So part of the question of what's "best" is the question of what's going to happen to you and Todd. Will you stay together, or break apart? The answer is that nobody knows for sure.

If you look beyond the immediate future, you see two lifestyles to choose from. One follows what I call "the ethic of intimacy." It says, "If two people love each other and are serious about each other, they should have intercourse." The ethic of intimacy tells you to practice sex with care and love in a relationship that's deeply meaningful.

In practice it means, for most people, a series of sexual partners. Take you and Todd as more or less typical examples. You've already had one partner each. Presumably you each got involved because you thought you were in love. That love fell apart, though, and you've escaped a bad relationship. Now you think, for the second time, you've found the right person to spend life with. Will you be correct this time? Or wrong again?

There are some signs against you. One is your youth. You're likely to change over the next few years. Going along with that is the fact that you'll probably be separated through his college years. Finally, you're both on the rebound from

LOVE, SEX & THE WHOLE PERSON

bad relationships. As anybody can tell you, your emotions are unreliable at such a time.

What's most against you, though, is that nothing besides your feelings binds you together.

Romantic love is inherently unstable. You don't know why you fall in love with someone in the first place, and it's equally hard to know why you stop liking him later. At one moment the mere sight of his face makes your heart stop; at the next you get irritable just hearing his voice droning on the phone. It's unpredictable. We go up and down, in and out, slaves to the whims of our feelings. Most people fall in love half a dozen times or more in the course of their lives.

So while there's a possibility that you and Todd will end up married happily ever after, there's a greater possibility that you won't. There's a high statistical probability that you'll end your relationship to him and go on to others. And naturally, since you'll be in love with these others too, you'll have sex with them. If you did it with him, you will have no reason to stop with others. Eventually, you'll probably settle down with one, live together for a time, and then get married. That's the pattern many people live by today. Is it "best"? Of course, it isn't. Let me give three reasons:

1. *It lowers the value of sex.* Sexual intercourse becomes a loving activity between two people—good, but lacking the high charge that comes with it when it is reserved for just one—the one you'll spend your life with.

2. *It blurs the distinction between married and unmarried.* You'll notice that many women's magazines have stopped referring to husband and wife. Instead they use terms like "partner" or "lover." Love is the big thing. Marriage is almost an afterthought. But love is hard to define; your feelings change. Marriage is something solid, clear, and definable that can protect your relationship from the ups and downs of your own feelings.

3. *It reduces your opportunity for the deepest kind of intimacy.* Sex is more than a physical act; it has a spiritual dimension, whether you want it to or not. When you have sex, something happens. You are not the same person any more;

you have been "one" with your partner, and you can never completely lose that oneness. When you then rip apart from that person, you carry a little bit of his or her personality stuck to yours. After you've been glued to half a dozen, the possibility for intimacy lessens. If you're like Hugh Hefner, with over a thousand partners, there's almost no imprint made at all. You probably can't even remember each person's name. The more partners you have, the less intimacy you experience. You may still marry, but it will be without the same level of self-surrender. Marriage means less and therefore offers less.

The other lifestyle, the one I'm committed to and the one I believe the Bible teaches, stakes everything on marriage. You look forward to the day when you give yourself completely to another person in total self-surrender. You count on that one relationship to give the security and stability you need for total intimacy. You save yourself for it. And when you finally do marry, more than your feelings bind you together. Your complete commitment, your absolute determination, bind you. So do the support of your family and your community and your church—for you were married in a public celebration and made promises before God "till death do you part."

How does this apply to you and Todd?

I don't know you—whether you're mature or immature, stable or unstable. But I can predict fairly confidently that you'll go through plenty of ups and downs in your relationship with Todd. That's normal. Maybe you'll make it through them and someday marry. Maybe you won't. If you do marry, I'm certain it's "best" for you to face that day with the sheer excitement and joy of the first time together. It's better to have waited for sex—to take your wedding day as a moment in time when you give yourself without reservation, forever. There's a peak joy in such a wedding that you just don't get if you've been sleeping together for some time. It's worth waiting for. It's the best of all possible beginnings.

And if you don't marry? If you break apart? I'd say it's

best for you to go on to other friends, including your future husband, without bits of Todd stuck unforgettably to you.

How could sex be immoral if we really love each other?

Q: I'm fifteen and my boyfriend is sixteen. Neither one of us is a virgin. In both cases it was something that couldn't be helped and was never intended. We are both strong Christians, which is something I am very happy about.

But I am struggling with one thing. We both feel that sex is something for two people who love each other. We plan to get married after college, but for now we're facing another problem: sex! We both feel that for us sex would be making love. And since we really love each other it wouldn't be wrong. The Bible says to stay away from sexual immorality. Since we really love each other, sex wouldn't be immoral. Is this wrong?

A: I believe you've reached a very serious misunderstanding. You're not alone. It's very widely believed today that the real message of Christianity is love, and that anything done in love cannot be immoral.

This is half right, and half right is especially dangerous for high-risk matters—folding parachutes or building relationships, for instance. Here's the part that's right: Love really is the greatest commandment. Jesus put love above every other rule for living. He was talking, though, about something quite different from the love you describe. Jesus gave the ultimate example of his kind of love when he died for his enemies. His love was for God and for his neighbor—a far cry from a romantic feeling. When you clean up after your little brother, you're "making love" with the love Jesus commanded. When you befriend a friendless person, you're "making love" in Jesus' way.

"Making love" with your boyfriend is an entirely different subject. That's not to put down what you and your boyfriend feel. Romance is wonderful. When you feel it, you want to act in genuinely self-sacrificing ways. Romantic love should go hand in hand with Jesus-style loving. But it certainly doesn't always do so, especially in the long run. If you were to talk seriously to half a dozen divorced couples (or even half a dozen high-school ex-couples), you'd find out that people who start out making romantic love in the tenderest way often end up hurting each other in a way that neither one ever forgets. That, I'm sure, is not the kind of love Jesus commanded.

The hard thing is to make romantic love go together with Jesus-style love and learn to keep them together for a lifetime. That's the key to deciding whether anything you and your boyfriend do is "moral" or "immoral." Does it lead toward a lifetime of Jesus-style love? Or does it lead away from it? Does it build you both up? Or does it tear you both down?

I believe that sex before marriage usually tears people down. True, relationships that include premarital sex do sometimes work out. And parachutes that are incorrectly folded do sometimes open. But should you risk your life on that?

Statistics from Rolling Stone Press's extensive survey *Sex and the American Teenager* show that only 14 percent of teenagers' sexual relationships last more than a year—about the same percentage that last a week. Almost all these kids go on to have sexual relationships with other partners. So by the time they marry, if they ever do, most have had quite a series of people they loved and went to bed with. Even though the majority of the girls said they originally planned to marry the guy they had sex with (the guys, more realistically, were less committed), the actual result was not lifelong love, but one broken sexual relationship after another.

Even if none of these kids got herpes or chlamydia or AIDS (millions do), and even if none of the girls got pregnant (millions do), and even if the two really did feel loving toward each other at the time, I can't believe that they found the best way to handle sex. There is just too much pain.

And do these experienced kids make the best candidates for marriage later on? I doubt it very much. I think they're good candidates for divorce. They're used to breaking up.

Another letter arrived in my mailbox recently. It read:

> I am a twenty-two-year-old female who, after dating someone for nine months, got engaged. After four months of being engaged, I broke off my engagement when I realized my fiancé was not what he had claimed to be.
>
> After we became engaged many people indicated that it was OK to be sexually involved because, after all, we were engaged, right? Wrong. I am so very glad we didn't go ahead with a sexual relationship because now I have nothing to regret.
>
> You never know where your relationship will go. If someone had told me that my former fiancé and I would not really be getting married, I'd have told them they were nuts.

I don't know this woman, nor her fiancé. I do know that their case isn't terribly unusual. For every couple that gets to the altar, there are several that "planned on being married" and never were. Being engaged is no guarantee. "Planning on marriage" is even less a guarantee.

Is premarital sex immoral? It certainly doesn't feel immoral. It feels good, and loving. But as far as I'm concerned, anything that keeps you from the full joy God intended is immoral.

Let me quote from one more letter:

> It really is hard being a teenager with a strong desire for sex. Especially once you've found that wonderful person that you want to share the rest of your life with. It's difficult to wait, I know. But with God's help,

and a man who loves the Lord, I was able to wait for the precious gift of sex.

Last month we celebrated our first wedding anniversary, and we are thankful to God for giving us the best year of our lives. We think that the fact that we waited has a lot to do with our present happiness and fulfillment. I hope this story can encourage others to wait until marriage. Even though it may seem impossible, it's well worth the wait.

What if we plan to marry as soon as it's economically possible?

Q: Derek and I have been dating for three-and-a-half years. Both he and I were virgins when we met—"innocent" virgins, not just technical. We're both juniors in college. Ours is not a rushed-into, fly-by-night relationship. It is a relationship that began as friends and Bible-study partners and blossomed into real love and commitment. Marriage is definitely in the future. We would like to spend the rest of our lives together, growing with and in Christ. But due to economic conditions and the fact that we're both putting ourselves through relatively expensive colleges completely by ourselves, there is no feasible way for us to get married until at least one of us is out of college.

The problem—an all-too-common one—is sex. We've been sleeping together for six months. I've been at a Bible college for three years and really desire to serve God. I know what he says about premarital relations, and I've studied the Bible enough to know that when God says something he has a reason for it. I read your column and I like what you have to say about the dangers of sex outside of marriage. I heartily agree. But they just don't seem to apply here.

Derek and I are not "just experimenting" and we're not having sex to "prove our love." (Only a lifetime of love and commitment will do that.) Sex is for us, as you have said, a unity of not only our bodies and minds, but our spirits. I won't get pregnant, and we are both in it to please the other as much as ourselves.

Yet the Bible does not seem to allow for any exceptions. I love Derek, but we love God more. If we could find a logical reason not to sleep together, we would stop. But I'm tired of hearing, "God said it, I believe it, that settles it." God gave us rational minds, and a statement like that doesn't show faith— only blind stupidity. If God doesn't want me to sleep with Derek, I need to know why.

A: I agree, to a point. Legitimate questions—and yours are legitimate—can be choked off by an appeal to blind faith. We cannot understand everything in life, and sometimes we have to simply obey God without understanding why. But that should not keep us from continuing to ask questions while we obey. Sometimes, when you persist with a question that seems impertinent to others, you break through to a new and deeper understanding of the love of our Father. Our rational minds were made for that very thing.

In trying to answer your questions, please pardon me if some questions pop into my mind about your relationship with Derek. I receive hundreds of letters from people in and out of love, and a large number say things like "We were so sure that it would last forever. Little did I know that. . . ." In reading these letters each month I trace the deep scars of those who were sure there would be no disease, no babies, no termination to their love. These letters have impressed me deeply with the high human potential for fooling ourselves. Hardly anybody who falls in love thinks it is just a brief fling, a purely physical attraction or an immature infatuation. They all think it is a deeply spiritual love that will last forever.

It's a good idea to remember the stuff we are made of and watch out for self-deception. When people are in love, very few are alive to their own weaknesses, or their partner's. Yet in love those weaknesses can hurt us as in almost no other relationship, for we are very tender when in love.

However, for now I'll take your word about you and Derek. You are going to be married. In a sense, you think you already are, for you have been bonded together by love. Why shouldn't you enjoy the full physical and spiritual intimacy of sex? Isn't that more appropriate than the struggle for sexual self-control you would undoubtedly experience if you tried to stay out of bed?

To answer that, I have to ask what sex is for. What did God mean it to be? In what role does sex really make people happy? My answer is that sex is the essential expression of love between a man and a woman who are totally together. They share everything; they hold nothing back psychologically, physically, materially, spiritually. In this complete embrace each one puts his or her partner's interests above his own. A marriage ceremony should be a celebration, a party to joyfully tell the world that, under God, two people have decided to make this all-or-nothing commitment. In that context sex is wonderfully appropriate.

No really significant commitment can be made halfway. Commitments are yes or no, all or nothing. When the pastor marries you, he asks whether you make this total commitment of love. You have to say yes. "Maybe" will not do.

Even lesser commitments are the same. When you buy a car, you have to put your money down; you don't take the car and think about it. If you try out for a sport, the coach wants to know if you are really serious; you can't show up for practice some days and forget about it other days.

But that is what you are trying to do with Derek. The very nature of sex is all-or-nothing. And yet you can't totally share your lives if you are at different colleges. Sharing means sleeping in the same bed, paying the same bills, deciding on the same furniture, eating breakfast at the same table. You can't do that. And why not? Because your college education is more important to you. You say you can't marry, but it's pretty obvious that you could, if you were willing to go to school one at a time. Sure, that's inconvenient. It may even be unwise, if you both want to get degrees. But don't you see what you're saying? On the one hand, you're saying, "We're totally committed. Nothing can tear us apart." And on the other hand, you let an inconvenient educational schedule tear you apart. You're much more committed to education than to each other. I can assure you, I wouldn't let economic sacrifices keep me from *my* wife.

Your commitment to each other is for tomorrow, not today. And commitments for tomorrow are notoriously weak. If you've ever sold a used car, you know you must never trust someone who says, "I'll bring the money tomorrow."

Look at another sign with me. You'll probably agree that a natural, healthy commitment of love is no secret. The world knows about it. This is true at any level of commitment. If a guy wants to take you out but makes you swear that you'll never tell his friends he likes you, it's a suspicious sign, to say the least. If two people are married but want the world to think they are just friends, they are either up to something illegal, or they are sick.

So what keeps you from making your all-or-nothing love public, which is the healthy and natural thing? I suspect the answer is public opinion.

You let public opinion deter you from expressing your love for each other in the most natural and healthy way. You prefer to live in secret because you don't want to face the consequences that would result if your unorthodox choice became known. I don't blame you for that. I just point out that your love isn't totally committed. You're halfway there, and halfway into a commitment is no commitment at all. In a genuine all-or-nothing love commitment, the kind sex was made for, nothing can tear you apart—not public opinion, not financial or educational inconvenience, not sickness or misfortune.

You've gone "all the way" physically but haven't gone "all the way" in commitment. The two should be synchronized, but they aren't in your case. Under such circumstances your relationship can begin to act like a car that has its timing off—starting and bucking and stopping, because all the parts aren't working together. People decry the increasing divorce rate. But what do you think the "divorce rate" is for couples like you and Derek?

I'm not saying your halfway commitment can't become a full commitment. It can, and I hope it does. But experience says it very well may not, and you'll reap a harvest of sadness, regret, and guilt.

You want to know what's wrong with what you're doing. I want to ask, "What's right about it?" God has given us a more joyful, secure way to total commitment. Why not listen to him?

Isn't what I do private, between me and God?

Q: I am a twenty-year-old girl who was a virgin until five months ago. My boyfriend, twenty-one, has had previous sexual relationships. I love him, and he loves me; there is no doubt of this. Marriage is a possibility. We would like to spend the rest of our lives together. But right now we're not financially ready for marriage because we are both in school.

I was always taught not to have sex before marriage. I thought I'd feel guilty if I ever did. But my boyfriend and I have been going to bed together for about five months, and I have no problems in my relationship with Christ. I know the Bible teaches sex before marriage is wrong. I also know that what is sin to one person may not be sin to the next.

I have often wondered if I'm fooling myself. It blows my mind that I have inner peace about my sex life. I am a leader in my college group, and I am considered a strong Christian. I don't feel bad for what I've done; I am glad. I realize sex drives are very strong and can get in the way of a relationship if you let them. But I've concluded, if you keep sex under control, your relationship can grow closer as long as it's all in perspective. The Lord, you, and your mate will just have to work it out. I guess my question is "Isn't sin up to individuals and their relationship with the Lord?"

A: Yes, to some extent you're right. In the Old Testament people relied on intermediaries (like Moses) to communicate with God. But Christians today can and must deal directly with God. We are responsible to him, and ultimately only to him, for the choices we make.

It's your application of this truth that troubles me. From your letter, it appears several things have convinced you that God wants you to have sex with your boyfriend:

"I love him and he loves me; there is no doubt of this."

"Marriage is a possibility."

"I have not once felt guilty."

"I have no problems in my relationship with Christ."

"I have inner peace."

"I don't feel bad for what I've done."

All this evidence boils down to the fact that you've had sex for five months and feel pretty good about it. No guilt. No problems with your boyfriend. No problems feeling good about God. You sound surprised about that, maybe because people who warned you about sex have stressed that you can find trouble in a hurry if you give in to temptation. Of course, you can. But you don't always.

I would call your rationale "existential." You are saying every person must decide on his own behavior, based on how he feels about it. This approaches Hemingway's famous statement: "Moral is what you feel good after; immoral is what you feel bad after."

You might be surprised to know I'll go along with that, as long as you make "after" include your whole life—now, in the future, and after your death. Unfortunately, it is pretty difficult to know at the age of twenty, and based on five months' experience, just what is going to make you happy by the time you're forty or seventy or sitting in front of God's judgment seat.

How can you be sure? Even your conscience is not totally reliable. You can fool it. And some people's consciences are more sensitive than others!

We can fool ourselves when we pray as well. The "answers" people receive from their prayers are not completely dependable. People get personal words from God that the world is ending tomorrow (it doesn't), that their baby brother is going to be healed (he isn't), that they should marry a certain girl (she won't).

Fortunately, God has not left us in the dark. He has given us some essential information for living—in the Bible. We are to check our consciences and answers to prayer against what the Bible says. You have already indicated that you know what it says about your situation.

Yes, sin is between you and God. And God has told you quite clearly that you are doing what he says is wrong. What you do about it is up to you.

What's wrong with a one-night stand?

Q: My problem is that at times I have such a strong sex drive that I want to make love to the first girl I see. I know this kind of lust is wrong, but I don't know what to do. I have tried praying, and I do well the first week, but thoughts that I shouldn't be thinking still come into my mind. I am writing also because I would like to know exactly what is wrong with a "one-night stand." I mean sex without any commitment. I know sex is a commitment of love between two married people, but I would still like to know a good reason and a passage I can look up in time of weakness.

A: Why no one-night stands? In other words, why does God make marriage so exclusive? Why can't we enjoy both casual sex and committed marriage, just as we enjoy potato chips and steak?

My answer is that there simply is no one-night stand. You cannot "love 'em and leave 'em." Casual, just-for-fun sex is as impossible as potato chips without calories. It's a pleasant-sounding idea, but it just doesn't exist.

This is because sex affects us to the core of our personalities. When that great, compelling urge is translated into action, whether in or outside of marriage, it changes things inside. For many, the act of sex comes like a blowtorch into their brain. The way they think about themselves, about the opposite sex, about sex itself, is never quite the same again.

Sex changes your relationship. You can never look at each other the same way again after that night. Even if you never see each other again, there is a relationship established that nags at the corners of your mind. You know that somewhere in the world a person exists who has, in the biblical sense, "known you." He or she owns a part of you.

I'd be the first to admit that these effects come in various forms. I have plenty of friends and acquaintances who have had numerous one-night stands but seem very untroubled by the experience. They don't feel guilty. They feel that it was a pleasant, exhilarating experience—a little like a carnival ride. They don't think they have been affected.

But I believe they have been affected. They have established a pattern. It will tend to extend itself through their lives.

You give yourself in sex; you put your ego on the line and present yourself to your partner. But a small gift you have given to a casual acquaintance is hard to turn into the gift of a lifetime to the one you have chosen to marry. It's hard to change your pattern of thinking on so basic a subject.

This is, I think, what Paul was getting at in 1 Corinthians 6:15–20: "Do you not know that someone who joins himself to a prostitute is one body with her? For God says, 'The two will become one flesh.'" You think you can walk away from a prostitute unchanged, because prostitution is the ultimate in the one-night stand. It's strictly a cash deal—no commitment, no emotion. But Paul says sex isn't like that. When two people have sex, they are deeply affected. And as Paul goes on to point out in the rest of the chapter, it affects very powerfully their relationships with God. As far as God is concerned, there is no one-night stand: your actions today eternally affect your relationship to him. How can God be "one" with someone who sins sexually and does not repent and ask forgiveness?

You're troubled by the immensity of your sex drive. Many of us are. It's hard work to keep your mind on the right track, and I don't know of any way to make it easy. Steering your sex drive is like steering a battleship: you have to think far ahead and be constantly alert.

Something so intense needs fulfillment. If the only fulfillment you get is in casual sex, you'll always be frustrated. You'll go from one partner to the next, always looking for something better. Sex strictly for pleasure is really just barely more pleasurable than masturbation. It is the love, the commitment, the joy, and the freedom you find in marriage that make sex so wonderful. This is what your powerful sex drive is pointing you toward.

Why not just live together?

Q: I'm a seventeen-year-old German girl and I'm getting *Campus Life* magazine every month as a gift. I read your column with great interest. You said in one of your recent answers that sex outside marriage is wrong.

Here in Germany it has become the fashion for young couples to live together without being married. I think they mostly do it out of honesty. They've just come to that conclusion because they still can't earn their own living (e.g., students, apprentices) or they just (if they are very young) want to learn whether they belong together at all. There's a big difference between going with someone and living with him.

An eighteen-year-old friend of mine is living with a guy who is twenty-two. But she doesn't feel guilty about it; most German girls wouldn't in her situation. She just feels too young to get married now, though that doesn't exclude the possibility they will get married sometime. Can you still say sex outside of marriage is wrong and consider her guilty? (I should add that in Germany, people don't care as much about the Bible as they do in America.)

A: Thank you for your thoughtful questions. America may not have gone so far as Germany in these attitudes, but we are not far behind. Your questions are terribly important. Christians must try to answer them.

Those around you believe that for many people, living together is best. It means you don't have to wait so long because of something trivial like money. And, most important, it means you can "back out" rather painlessly if things don't work out right. Anyone who has felt the pain of a divorce, either in his own family or through friends, can't help feeling that there ought to be a better way. Hence, "trial marriages."

Of course, many people aren't serious in their arguments for living together; they just want sex without attachments. But there are also a good many people who really believe that living together is best.

Living together may make sense, I think, for those willing to compromise their ideals about love. I think more and more people are looking at relationships between the sexes as a kind of dull necessity—sometimes wonderful, but more frequently painful. The best that they hope for is not to be hurt too badly, not to be taken in. So they live together, try to care for each other sincerely, and try not to interfere with each other's goals and plans. If this accommodation breaks down, they go their separate ways—the easier the departure, the better.

Judging by the standards of our day, I wouldn't say this is wrong. But as a Christian, I am not content to judge things by the standards of our day. God has proposed, in the Bible, a higher standard, one that he says will satisfy people who live by it.

But even apart from Christian standards, look more closely at the arguments people make for living together. They claim it will make the pain of divorce unnecessary. But if so, why does this "living together" society suffer more divorces than previous societies? They say those who live together marry only when they "really know" they fit together. But why do people who plan their marriages through this safe and sane trial method so frequently end up with failures on their hands? (Studies consistently show that "living together" couples fail more often at marriage than those who don't live together.) Nor does the freedom to live together seem to much diminish the pain when people separate. Living together makes sense . . . until you try it. In reality, it does not live up to its promise at all.

But there is a better alternative. Let me mention three proposals:

1. *You can best get to know another person without sex.* I know this is just the opposite of what many people think. But, in fact, sex is a heavily weighted, frequently confusing element in an uncommitted relationship. It does funny things. Sometimes it falsely satisfies their urge to "be one," and the probing energy of their relationship dies gradually (or even suddenly). They wake up one morning, and their relationship means nothing! Sex has not helped it to grow; it has hindered it.

2. *Sex is, by nature, a spiritual, lifelong commitment.* Sexual relationships are not like pieces of a jigsaw puzzle that can be assembled and pulled apart without damage. Sex is more like epoxy glue. Have you ever tried to mend some pottery after a failure on the first attempt? Once the glue has hardened on both pieces, they do not match right, and it is harder to bond them together. So it is with a broken sexual

relationship. A successful, lasting bond becomes less and less likely each time you start over.

3. *Marriage protects and nurtures love.* The way some people talk, you would think that marriage and love were opposites. But that is propaganda, spread through TV and movies and books by people who know nothing about committed love. The bond of Christian marriage—a pledge before God and friends that with their help you will never let any force break you apart—gives love the time, peace, security, and hope that it needs to grow. Marriage does not create love. Only the partners can do that. But it provides you with the maximum chance, and God makes clear that he will help. There is no reason why anyone need fail.

Many people assume that the main reason for marriage is to protect children. Thus people who are living together decide to get married only when they are ready to have children. Children do need protection from the harsh forces of the world, but they are not the only ones. Lovers need that protection too, and they find it only in pledging themselves to marriage.

Marriage is a risk—I don't mean to minimize that. No matter how well you know your partner, there is still plenty you don't know.

Living together is offered as a better, risk-free lifestyle. It isn't risk-free, and it isn't better. And it is far from God's best.

But won't God forgive us anyway?

Q: I'm going with a non-Christian guy, and the only thing that's stopped me from going to bed with him is the fact that I kind of want to stay a virgin. But isn't it true that God forgives and forgets? So what's wrong with it, if my God will still forgive me?

A: I guess you're asking a variation of the question posed in Romans 6:1: "Shall we go on sinning so that grace may increase?" A contemporary version is, "I enjoy sinning; God enjoys forgiving. Why can't we relate on that basis?"

Yes, it is true that God forgives and forgets—for those who are really sorry and willing to change. But to count on that in advance seems to imply a cynical outlook. If you will be really sorry, why do it in the first place? God is not a machine you punch your formulized prayer into for forgiveness. He is a Person. Would you casually steal from your mother, knowing she'd probably forgive you later?

If something is wrong, it's wrong whether it's later forgiven or not. God forgives murderers, too, and gossips and cat-torturers. But I wouldn't recommend any of those careers to you. Nor would I recommend that you sleep with your boyfriend. Even those who are sincerely sorry and are forgiven often find that the emotional scars they've gained stay for years. Sex is as personal as anything you ever do. It can affect you very deeply. It is not something you wipe away with the casualness of erasing a blackboard.

Let me add, although you haven't asked—your relationship with a non-Christian is in the wrong, too. First Corinthians 6:14 tells Christians not to be "yoked" together with non-Christians. In contemplating sex with this guy, you're involving yourself in the strongest "yoke" we know. (See the section on dating non-Christians for more information.)

But sex is an overwhelming drive!

Q: I am a Christian, even though you may find that hard to believe when you hear what I have to say. After taking "spiritual inventory" of my whole self, I find one area in which I am in direct conflict with the Bible and most of my Christian friends. That area is premarital sex. The way I see it, if God had intended sex only for marriage, he would have made the sex drive start at marriage and not before.

I probably won't get married for a while, but I have an overwhelming sex drive. The idea of relieving it through "sublimation" sounds like baloney to me. Sexual arousal is meant to find its release in orgasm, not in jogging, basketball, an invigorating game of tennis, or a modern dance class.

Christians tell me that I have the power of the Holy Spirit within me to resist sexual temptation. I must be missing out on something. I don't seem to harbor any great reservoirs of power in my soul.

A: I agree that relieving the sexual drive through "sublimation" isn't terribly effective. But I don't think your picture of the sex drive is very accurate, either.

You picture the sex drive as a physical need that gets stronger every minute. It's like a reservoir of steam, building pressure until it explodes. I don't think that's the way sex is at all. A sex drive never "overwhelms" anyone.

Sex is not a need, like hunger, but a drive (like curiosity, or the desire for approval) that requires direction. It isn't satisfied by having sex any more than by sublimation. Quite the opposite; it's aroused. The more you have sex, the more day-to-day conscious of sex you are. (Perhaps this is why you find your drive overwhelming.)

As a rule, those able to thank God for their sexuality (that is, for the fact that they are men or women, attracted to the opposite sex), yet control themselves, are the people least driven by sex. Jesus would be my prime example. The only man who truly "had it all together" had a full sex drive (he was fully human) but never fulfilled it in intercourse. And he was certainly not repressed or inhuman. He was warm, caring, directed, fulfilled.

It's not easy to wait. But whoever suggested that the best

way to live is the easiest? In every area of life, it's the exceptional effort that brings exceptional results.

You ask where the power of the Holy Spirit is in your life. But that is something you won't ever know until you rely on it. God doesn't turn us into invulnerable supermen, with power we are absolutely sure could never be overcome. He only promises enough strength to do what we need to do, when we need it.

You may not feel that power inside, at least not as a spiritual surge in your gut. The Holy Spirit isn't mainly interested in giving surges to our gut. His first concern is to teach us what is true. When faced by a decision, we can know "this is right—and best for me."

Beyond that, the Holy Spirit wants to give us a new character, so that we are able to say no (and yes) even when the pressure is to do the opposite. But you won't feel that new strength until you begin to rely on God to give it to you. Until you come to the point where you want to go against the pressure of our society, you won't be able to experience God's help in doing so.

How can we be sure we're sexually compatible?

Q: I am nineteen years old, and have been dating the same boy for three years. Even after spending a year at separate colleges, we are still very much in love. We are both Christians and have talked to a great extent about sex. We both feel it is an area in our lives that God wants us to share only in marriage—whether with each other or with someone else. I have always been set in my beliefs about sex before marriage, and not until lately did I think twice about it.

My question was aroused in a child-development class I am taking. The professor is very neutral on the topic of sex

LOVE, SEX & THE WHOLE PERSON

before marriage, but did bring up an interesting story. It was about a couple who had waited until marriage to engage in sexual intercourse. After they had experienced it, they found that they could not please each other sexually.

I know that through steady dating and engagement we learn a lot about our future spouses, but what about the sexual side?

As for me, I want marriage to be a one-shot deal, and before I make my vows I want to be sure I'm marrying the perfect guy in all ways. I realize that God has someone special for me, but does this mean he will be adequate and perfect in this area, too, along with the rest? Or will I be perfect for him?

I know that sex isn't the basis for a good marriage, but it is a part, and I want mine to be beautiful—as God made it to be. So is it wrong to have premarital sex when you're approaching marriage?

A: When people talk about sexual incompatibility, it often sounds like a mechanical or medical fact—as though people were sexually incompatible the way a Chrysler transmission is incompatible with a Toyota engine. But I have never heard of people being sexually incompatible in that sense. Couples may have a poor sex life, but it almost never has anything to do with some unchangeable fact. If you want to test physical sexual compatibility, you can both go to a doctor and ask him to examine you. That will give you better information than trying it out for yourselves.

What makes sex good between people is not something physical, but something extremely changeable: the quality of their relationship, their individual self-acceptance, and their relaxed and accepting attitude toward sex.

Although people dream about their honeymoon, for many it is sexually disappointing. They're tense. They're inexperienced. Things really get humming only long after the honeymoon. Many people say it takes about five years of marriage to begin to experience peak sexual satisfaction.

Change can go the other way, too. There have been many reports of people who enjoyed sex while dating and then, when they were married, didn't. There are plenty of cases of people who had wildly ecstatic sexual experiences soon after they met but whose sexual relationship quickly deteriorated to nothing.

One implication is that it is impossible to test your sexual happiness in advance. If you do test, the test is very likely to come out negative, because many people don't have a great first time (or second, third, or fourth) in bed.

The only real "test" is to know each other, to talk freely, to develop the kind of relationship that sees into each other. It is a good idea to talk about sexual expectations while you are engaged so that you can become more relaxed with each other and understand each other's attitudes better. Premarital counseling, too, can often probe helpfully into sexual attitudes and expectations.

Sexual compatibility isn't the problem. Be concerned about compatibility, period—human compatibility. Sex is a creative venture you experience with your partner. It takes security, love, care, and gentleness, and especially it takes patience. When things are not going well, that doesn't mean you should divorce. It means you should give more attention to practice!

Won't our wedding night be embarrassing if we're virgins?

Q: I have a question that's baffled my friends and me for months now. We all feel that sex before marriage isn't right, but there's one problem that makes us think twice. I feel that if my husband's not a virgin when we marry, and I am, it would be a disaster the first time we make love. He will know exactly what to do, and I will be making trips to the library, reading books and trying to learn. That's what makes us want to become "experienced" before our wedding night so we can satisfy our husbands. Several close male friends of mine all say they want their wives to know exactly what to do so they won't have to teach them. (And these are Christian friends!) Please help us figure this out so we can put our minds at ease and relax on our wedding night.

A: I doubt that anybody is relaxed on his or her wedding night. Are you supposed to be relaxed on the most wonderful day of your life? I'd prefer the word *excited*.

However, I think I can put your mind at ease. First of all, being a virgin hardly guarantees a sexual disaster on your wedding night. Actually, it's terrific to be a virgin. Learning about sex with the person you love most in the world can be exciting.

Your sexual technique may be clumsy, but the fact that you're giving yourself in a way that you've never given yourself before more than makes up for it. Where there is no experience, there are also no comparisons. After a married couple have been to bed with each other a thousand times they're likely to become much better at technique, and they're also likely to become a lot more relaxed with each other. Sex does get better. Still, there's no time like the first time. Mistakes are hilarious (at least they are afterwards) and always very tender. I hate to think that anyone would deliberately waste this wonderful, frightening, earth-shaking experience on anyone but the one they love so much they want to stay together forever.

Second, you seem overly worried about making the first night wonderful. You should worry more about the nights two and three and twenty years later. No doubt a sexually experienced person is smoother the first night. (Though not always so delightful.) But will he or she be so skilled at making love stay alive? In general the more sexually experienced a person, the less able they are to "bond" for life. See Hollywood for examples.

Third, being experienced is not as big a help as you think. It's like being an experienced onion peeler. It doesn't mean you're good at peeling tomatoes. Each vegetable is different. Each human being's sexual enjoyment is different. You have to learn what turns that particular person on. Typically, a married couple need years to really thoroughly understand each other's bodies. And even after that, there's a lot more learning to be done.

Anyway, good sex is only partly related to good sexual technique. Much more important is the security, the love, the tenderness of a person who you know will never leave you. In an insecure, uncaring environment sex is often not so great. Some "sexually experienced" people think they have learned all there is to know about sex. But what they've experienced is really inferior, because it wasn't founded on love that lasts forever.

So forget about experience. I can promise you that the only difference being a virgin on your wedding day will make is a positive difference.

"I wish I'd waited!"

Q: Like so many people who have written to you, I intended to wait until after marriage to have sex. But then I met this one particular guy who became very special to me. We dated each other for a year and a half, and for the first twelve months I resisted all of the physical "pressure" he put on me. I explained again and again that I wanted to wait, but eventually I gave in. I can make all kinds of excuses for what happened—I was having a very hard time accepting my parents' divorce, and I felt very lonely—but that doesn't change the facts. Of course, at that time we "loved" each other and were planning marriage, and I didn't think it really mattered too much.

I'm sure you can guess the outcome. Not very long after

we made love, he decided he didn't "love" me anymore; then we broke up. The guilt and hurt that I experienced lasted nine months. During those months I had to talk to many understanding friends to try to learn to forgive myself and to get over caring for him so much. But even now I still experience a twinge of pain that, as you've said, will never completely go away.

It's a hard way to learn the truth. I had a lot of good advice that I never bothered to listen to. I just never thought my situation would end that way. Now I know all too well that once you start getting physical, finding a "good stopping place" before going all the way is almost impossible. I've learned, too, that at age seventeen I really didn't know anything at all about the true, lasting love that comes from a deep commitment. Now, at eighteen, I still can't comprehend the perfect love that will come in marriage.

Please print my letter. I know that your readers have heard the same advice from you again and again, but maybe my experience will influence someone not to be sexually involved before marriage. I didn't listen, but now I know: the pain of ending a relationship tied up with sex is much worse than ending one without it. Sex is meant to bind two people together forever. I feel like I've lost a part of me to him that will never return, and can never be replaced. I hope someone else will be able to learn without undergoing the harsh lesson themselves.

A: Thanks to your letter, maybe some will. Thank you for writing.

Q: I'm writing in response to the fifteen-year-old Christian girl who wrote telling you she and her boyfriend don't feel guilty about having sex. When I was fourteen, the same thing happened. My boyfriend and I both attended a Christian high school, and we knew premarital sex was wrong, but we loved each other and felt it only deepened our relationship. Many times we tried to "quit," but it never lasted, and our relationship got . . . stronger? Well, maybe, if stronger means his demands on me to have sex in the worst settings, with less and less consideration of my feelings. But when our relationship became rocky, and he wanted to break up, I couldn't bear the thought of *my* boyfriend being shared with someone else.

Well, we stuck it out, and when I was eighteen, he nineteen, we married. We never fought or argued (the only thing we had argued over before was sex), just lived together without guilt, but also without respect for each other's feelings. We had lost that years ago. And sex was no big deal because that sacredness was thrown out the window.

Did you ever eat too much cookie dough, and when the cookies were baked, you didn't want any?

Well, with all those years of rejecting God's law of purity, after one year of marriage, my husband left me and moved in with a girl he worked with. It wasn't until then— until I sat alone, rejected, pregnant, and burned by the fire I had kindled—that I finally understood why the Bible says to *wait*. Why would a man (or woman) honor God by keeping a marriage covenant when we couldn't honor him (and each other) before marriage? We surely reap what we sow.

A: Thank you for sharing your experience, as dreadful as it is. Your letter is a frightening reminder that we're really not playing a game. Our lives are made by our choices. I hear from many people who are making choices about their sexual lives; I rarely receive such a sobering account of where those choices can lead.

Yet I can't completely agree with your last sentence. We don't have to reap what we sow, though by all that's natural we should. The Christian message is good news: Jesus reaped all the death and destruction we sow for ourselves. He died for us, so that we could escape from the normal consequences of our choices. I feel for you as you describe your sense of well-deserved desperation. I don't have any magic to make it all right. The pattern you established, which took five years to reach its conclusion, may take even longer to be made right. Yet, in God's mercy it can be made right. He loves you. He cares for you. And, most important, he forgives all who seek his forgiveness. There is a new beginning. You do not have to reap what you sow. You can reap what *Jesus* sows.

"I'm glad I waited!"

Q: I'm twenty-four years old, and I've been reading your column on and off since I was in high school. I still subscribe to *Campus Life*, partly to show me how much I've grown, and partly to remind me how much I've yet to grow.

I'm a teacher in an elementary school and I work with teenagers. I save your column and a few other articles so I have a reference. I think the hardest thing for the kids to believe about me is that I'm still a virgin. I always tell them it's a lot harder to say no to sex than it is to say yes to sex.

Most of my friends, both male and female, are not virgins. Many of them wish that they had waited until marriage to have sex. Not that they don't love their spouses or fiancés. It's just that it would have made sex more special. The friends who did wait are glad they did.

I try to pass this on because I know it's hard; believe me, I know. But when I break up with a guy and I'm hurting, deep down it helps knowing that I have no regrets about our physical relationship.

A: Thanks for the encouragement and for putting the value of your virginity in believable terms. In reading your letter, I was struck afresh by the difference in approach between what the Bible offers and what non-Christians think it offers.

Many non-Christians see the world as a beautiful, green field with a few deep, dangerous holes to avoid. Seeing things that way, they think Christians have labeled sex outside of marriage as one of those deep, dangerous holes. That's their quarrel with us, for they can see with their own eyes that people who have sex before they're married don't disappear down a hole. Rather, they often carry on with life more or less like everybody else. Their logical conclusion is that sex outside of marriage must not be a deep, dangerous hole. Christians must be wrong.

But they misunderstand the Christian message. The Bible does portray the world, as God made it, as a beautiful, green field. But we're not cavorting about that field. We've already fallen down a hole. In fact the whole human race was born in a hole, because of our deep, stubborn rebelliousness against God. It shows in the anger, jealousy, broken promises, selfishness, and malice that so often permeate our lives and our thinking. As to our sexuality, it's "in a hole" too, as shown by broken relationships, jealousy, infidelity, loneliness, and lovelessness.

Jesus Christ came into the world to enable us to escape that hole. As for our sexuality, he wants us to become people capable of the deeply committed, spontaneously joyful, delightedly naked relationship that Adam and Eve enjoyed. But to get there is not easy. We can never make it on our own. And there are certain activities that interfere with a person's attempt to rise out of muck. Sex outside marriage is one. When you do it, you don't fall down a hole. You *stay* down the hole. You're likely to continue with the ordinary, semi-committed, what's-in-it-for-me kind of relationships. You're less likely to rise to the kind of love that lasts forever.

God wants sex to be better. He made it for our pleasure. He made it to be the seal of a totally committed, loving, secure, lifelong, exclusive relationship—the kind of love affair that goes by the name of Christian marriage. It's no doubt true that nobody on this earth has lived up to the ideal God wants us to experience. Christians struggle with all kinds of forces that drag them down. Some people, however, are moving in the right direction. Others are content to stay in their hole. I'm glad to hear that your choice is toward something more "special" than the ordinary experience of sexuality. It's not easy, as you say. It's always easier to stay where you are. It takes energy to rise. And God, by his Spirit, offers all the help we need.

6. *Masturbation*

What does the Bible say about masturbation? Is it a sin?

Q: I am eighteen years old and a virgin. The problem is, to release my sexual tension, I masturbate. Many times I have tried to quit, but I always start again. This could get a bit embarrassing when I go to college and share a dorm room. I wanted to hear your thoughts. Are there Bible verses that preach against it? If so, how could I quit without ending up losing my virginity because of my pent-up passion?

A: You've asked for my thoughts, and that's what I'll give you. Unfortunately, though I've thought about masturbation for many years, I've never been able to get my thoughts totally into focus. I'll share with you what I know. Some of it may help you. Some of it will leave you still wondering—as I still do.

You may find it helpful to know, first off, that as surely as I'm alive these words are being read with avid attention and acute embarrassment all over America. Every poll I've ever seen shows that most kids masturbate. It's more frequently a concern among guys than among girls, but both sexes stimulate themselves to orgasm. Beside that, hundreds and hundreds of kids who have written me have said that masturbation causes more than "a little embarrassment." Most feel intensely guilty. Every time they do it, they loathe themselves. Not everyone masturbates, and not everyone who does feels guilty about it. But that's the way it is for the majority.

So you're not the only one. Most of the kids you know probably feel the same way you do—whether they're virgins or not. I hope that fact reduces any self-hatred you feel. You're not especially rotten. You're just average.

The second fact I want you to know is that the Bible says nothing about masturbation. It's not because of delicacy. The Bible comments on a wide variety of sexual activity, from intercourse with animals to intercourse with members of the same sex. But it offers not a word on masturbation.

That's not to say the Bible has nothing relevant to say. God offers us words of wisdom about lust, about mental self-control, about purity of life. Most people who believe masturbation is sin will quote the Bible on these subjects, and they have a point. Masturbation is usually accompanied by sexual fantasies. I don't think there's anything necessarily wrong with thinking about sex, but I do think a person's sexual imagination needs to be controlled. Most people who masturbate harbor fantasies that are plainly immoral. These should have no place in a Christian's life.

So it's puzzling why masturbation goes unmentioned in the Bible. Could it be that people in those times didn't masturbate? I find that highly unlikely. I can only conclude that masturbation is much less significant to God than it is to most of us. A lot of young Christians, if they were truthful, would put masturbation as the most significant battle line in their attempt to live as Christians. God does not, apparently, consider it even worth mentioning. I don't completely understand why that is so, but I suspect it may have something to do with my next point.

The third "fact" about masturbation is one I can't prove but believe quite firmly: masturbation doesn't affect your life in any dramatic way, good or bad.

You've alluded to one theory about the *positive* effects masturbation can have: the theory that masturbation relieves your sexual tension and thus allows you to stay a virgin. I haven't seen any evidence that masturbation makes such a difference. Of course masturbation does temporarily relieve sexual tension, but that doesn't mean it changes your basic sexual urges. Sexual passion is not like a steam boiler whose pressure must occasionally be released. Sexual passion is a fundamental drive that must be channeled into a way of life. If masturbation makes any difference in that choice, it's a very minor one.

In other words, if you were to quit masturbating, I don't think it would make it any more difficult to stay a virgin. According to one survey I've seen, those who are sexually promiscuous masturbate just about like everyone else. Masturbation doesn't remove their interest in sex.

On the negative side, some people wonder whether masturbation will ruin them for marriage. Will they develop sexual patterns that will inhibit them later on? Will their guilt and self-loathing make them into unhappy marriage partners? Again, I have yet to see evidence that it's so. Some individuals do experience such problems. But perhaps their difficulties are just part of their personality makeup. I would guess that in 90 percent of all happy marriages, one or both of the partners have masturbated. I would guess that in 90 percent of all terrible marriages, one or both of the partners have masturbated. On the whole, I don't see that masturbation has much effect.

The fourth fact about masturbation is that quitting is very, very difficult. All sexual patterns are difficult to change, and masturbation, because it's so private, may be the most difficult of all. Some people try to make themselves quit by emphasizing what a horrible, filthy thing they have done. They think that if they could make themselves feel the absolute depths of guilt and degradation, it would help them stop. This strategy doesn't work, so don't try it. You probably feel bad enough without trying to make yourself believe you're worse than you really are. If masturbation is no big deal to God, it shouldn't be for you.

Over the years I've asked readers of my column to write and tell me what helped them quit masturbating. Out of the hundreds of thousands who read my column each month, only a dozen or so have written. Most of these have said that emphasizing God's love and the power of his Holy Spirit helped them most of all—not their sense of sin and degradation.

If you're like most people, you'd like to quit masturbating. I'd certainly encourage you to try. But I'd also warn you that you may not be able to. I want you to know that if you can't stop, it won't ruin your life. God has many other far more significant concerns for your life. He would like you to grow in your relationships with other people, in your prayer and Bible study and worship, and in your obedience to his commands. If masturbation becomes more significant to you than these issues, you're off the track.

It's not an all-or-nothing battle. Even if you don't quit, you can begin to gain in self-control and in purity of thought. You may not become all you want to be, but you can become better than you are, with God's help. Most people have success in cutting down the frequency of their masturbation and in eliminating immoral sexual fantasies from their minds.

I'd strongly recommend talking to a friend about your struggles with masturbation. I know it's hard to do—to break out of your private guilt and frustration. But it helps tremendously to end that silence and to have someone able to pray for you and encourage you.

A lot of people want to know, "Is masturbation a sin?" I have to answer, in a most unsatisfying manner, "I don't really know." God's silence on the subject leaves me uncertain.

From a practical point of view, however, I'm not sure it matters whether we call it a sin or not. Whatever you call it, you would like to stop it. Whatever you call it, quitting is very difficult. Whatever you call it, it is not high on God's list of concerns—not so high as, say, gossip, or anger. Perhaps the most important thing I can say about masturbation is that while we human beings tend to see it as terrifically significant, God wants us to pay more attention to other things.

Is masturbation bad for you?

Q: I have been masturbating for approximately thirteen years. I'm now twenty-four years old. I don't remember why I started masturbating. Maybe it was because I had a Playboy centerfold or something. But I certainly agree with what you've written: it comes from impure thoughts and sexual fantasies.

I am a Christian, and have been for seven years. As a Christian, I felt guilty every time I masturbated. It felt good while in the act, but after I stopped I felt guilty and ashamed. I knew it was wrong and in direct disobedience to the Lord, yet I willfully did it. Up until this spring, when I told my spiritual counselor that I masturbated, I would always feel guilty. He told me that I had to stop feeling guilty about it, to accept God's forgiveness.

I am a virgin. I have pent-up sexual desires. Something that has helped me with my problem is that I met a young lady. Just meeting her helped me. It gave me the desire to want to stop. Just knowing her and developing a relationship with her as a friend have given me something else besides sexual fantasies and immoral thoughts to think about. I still do masturbate, off and on, but not anywhere near as often as I did. I hope you can publish this, and help someone else out.

A: I suspect the biggest help you or I or anybody has to offer is the plain acknowledgment that masturbation bothers a lot of people. It's a strange thing: even among people who talk nonstop about sex, masturbation is seldom mentioned. Some may eagerly describe in great detail who does what with whom, but they don't say much about the commonest sexual practice there is among young people. Nobody likes masturbation. People may say it's natural, but they don't talk as though it's natural.

Here are some reasons why:

1. *Masturbation is lonely.* The story of creation tells how God made male and female for each other's joy and friendship. Eve was made, the story says, because God found it "not good" for man to be alone (Genesis 2:18). Our sexuality is meant for making two people one. But when you masturbate, you are alone, and that feels "not good." The very best you could say for masturbation is that it's second-rate—less than what God meant us to experience sexually.

2. *For most people (not all) masturbation goes with sexual fantasies.* Since Jesus warned that lusting after a woman amounts to committing adultery with her "in the heart," a lot of people assume that their fantasies are evil. It's not quite as simple as that. The biblical word for "lust" really just means "strong desire," and the meaning is determined by the context. For instance, Jesus told his disciples at the Last Supper, literally, "I have lusted to eat this Passover with you before I suffer" (Luke 22:15). Clearly, lust isn't bad in that context, and it's also unlikely that Jesus is saying, "I've fantasized about having this Passover meal with you." Fantasy and lust are different, at least some of the time.

Some people think Jesus' words could be translated, loosely, "If you really wish you could do it and if you would do it if you wouldn't get caught, you're just as bad as the person who does it." That's obviously different from someone imagining anonymous Playboy bunnies when he's masturbating. He doesn't want to do anything with those bunnies in real life. They're just mental tools.

But having said that, I can't say much good about those mental movies of bunnies. A lot of people use pornography to masturbate—a kind of idol worship. A lot of people invent their own mental pornography. Their fantasies are usually loveless, depersonalized. In response to this, some people recommend that people try to imagine their wedding night, or some positive, hopeful sexual context. This sounds like a good idea, except that I'm not so sure it works. How do you imagine your wedding night, if you don't know whom you'll marry? And if you are engaged, won't those fantasies make waiting for the wedding harder?

I'm not sure that Jesus' comments on lust referred to exactly what goes on in people's minds when they masturbate. But I am sure that what goes on in most people's minds when they masturbate is far from ideal.

3. *Masturbation is often uncontrollable.* People try hard to stop, and they can't. They pray, plead, make resolutions, take cold showers, run five miles a day—and still do it. A lot of people, like you, have described to me their conviction that they were directly disobeying God's will when they masturbated. They seem to try to dig that into their minds, as a way of getting themselves psyched up to stop. It hardly ever works. Masturbation is just too powerful an impulse. Nobody likes that aspect of it. We like to think our lives are under our control, but masturbation often isn't.

Considering these three points, who would want to masturbate? And yet, people do. Christians are no exception, judging by all the evidence I've seen.

Many older people, including outstanding Christian psychologists, pastors, and theologians, have decided that masturbation is nothing to worry about, so long as it doesn't dominate your life. I think these Christian leaders reached their conclusions as they got older and looked back on their own masturbation. They felt that perhaps it wasn't as big an issue as it had seemed at the time.

That doesn't make them right. But they do raise some important points.

So what conclusions do I draw from all this? I'm more tentative than I'd like, but here's where I come down:

1. *Masturbation is second-rate, at best.* I'd like people to remember that God didn't make us male and female so that we could masturbate. He has something richer and more wonderful in mind.

2. *I don't call masturbation sin.* Who am I to say it's sin if God didn't? I think people do sin when they use pornography or deliberately stick to fantasies that are degrading or immoral. I also think that, because we're fallen creatures still far from God's ideal, our sexual fantasies usually are far from God's ideal. But I don't like the way people emphasize their

sinfulness in order to try to get themselves to stop masturbating. I don't think it helps them to stop. I think your spiritual counselor gave you good advice: stop feeling guilty, and accept God's forgiveness.

3. *I urge people to stop masturbating if they can, or at least to slow down.* How do you do that? The best technique I know is one you've stumbled on: stop thinking so much about yourself, including your masturbation. Get involved with people. Make some friends. Get involved with God. Praise him. Worship him. And don't do it only in order to quit masturbating. Do it because he's worth it, in himself, and make friends because other people are worth it, in themselves.

4. *I urge people who can't quit to stop worrying about it.* God has a lot of other things he would rather have you worry about. The Bible is full of them. Once you've learned to obey the commands that are written there, you can start working on the commands you think should have been included.

I remember very well how much energy, prayer, and agony I invested in this problem. I don't think it ever did me much good. I couldn't quit until I married. (Some people can't even quit then.) I wish I hadn't had to go through that.

But I did, and I survived intact. In fact, I did gain one thing from it. As wretched as I felt about myself, I learned that I was still beloved by God. Somehow, his amazing grace slipped through to my consciousness, even when I felt lower than green scum in the gutter. God gets through to us poor creatures with his love, and not even masturbation can stop him.

I masturbate. Do I have any right to be a camp counselor, since I can't control myself?

Q: I am a quite normal Christian in high school. I go to a Bible study, a youth group, and a prayer group before school, and I even plan to head a fellowship group at school next year. I have a lot of friends. But one terrible habit eats away at me night and day. I masturbate.

I plan to be a counselor to little kids at a camp next summer, and I wonder if I have a right to do it. I feel that if I can't control myself in private, it probably shows up when I'm in public. How I wish I could stop. I've considered asking my pastor for help, but he doesn't seem that sensitive. I want to ask a friend for help, but I'm not sure what he would think of me.

A: Nobody, but nobody, is proud of masturbation. It seems to serve as a magnet for self-loathing. Nothing is so intimate and personal as orgasm, but in masturbation you find yourself totally isolated, doing something to yourself that feels terrifically pleasurable physically, and terrifically repulsive emotionally. When I was your age, the very mention of the word could make me blush.

Yet masturbation is so hard to quit. Clearly some people can and do quit masturbating—but for everyone who quits, there must be hundreds who can't. Considering the agony I am sure you and hundreds of thousands of others put into your efforts to quit, the results do not seem very encouraging.

Why am I telling you this? Not to prove that there's nothing wrong with masturbation. Certain kinds of habits rule us far more strongly and irrationally than others. Smoking, drinking, overeating—habits of the mouth—can be murder to break. Habits of sex can be even harder. That doesn't make them right.

I am telling you this because I believe, frankly, that some realism is called for. Whatever we say about masturbation, let's make sure we keep in mind the real-life experience of hundreds of thousands of people. Whether we call masturbation sinful or not, nine out of ten people would, if they could, gladly quit. The problem is, nine out of ten try to quit and fail.

It is here that the question "Is masturbation a sin?" has relevance.

Does it mean that if you can't quit you have ruined your relationship with God? I don't think so. I think we must accept the fact that while we sin in many ways, some ways we don't even know about, the sins God wants to confront us on are those he has named in the Bible.

An inner impression may have convinced you that God wants you to quit, and I will not argue with that. It's important to listen to our consciences. But we do not build our lives around inner impressions. We build our lives around God's will revealed in the Bible. Any other source of guidance is incomplete and unreliable. You can count on this: God is not going to throw you out of his house because you can't quit masturbating. If he cared that way about it, he would have told us so.

For me, it comes down to a question of priorities. If you want to quit, keep trying. You'll be happier if you succeed. But since this is not God's high priority, I don't think it is right to exert every spiritual muscle, every prayer, every thought to the job of quitting.

God's enemies want to make you discouraged, hopeless, frustrated, spending all your time and energy on an issue you can't master and ignoring the really important concerns of God. The greatest tragedy would be if masturbation left you feeling totally worthless, cast off from God, dirty. If you retreated in frustration from relationships with God or with friends, if you developed a pattern of thinking that sex is disgusting and shameful, if you became preoccupied with masturbation—that, I believe, would break God's heart.

So don't let your concern over one area of your life dominate the rest of it. The Bible studies and other activities you are involved in are nothing but good.

You need not be ashamed to help others just because you masturbate. If that disqualified you, we would have few leaders. Feel free to throw yourself into Christian activities. And concentrate on God's bigger issues: worship of him, love for your neighbor, generosity toward the poor, finding true fellowship with other Christians.

Masturbation will be something that fades out of your life as you get older. It will do you no permanent harm. At least, that has been my experience and the experience of many others. And if it were not so, God would have told us.

How can I quit masturbating, or at least manage my "habit"?

Q: I feel angry at myself and at the devil. Why? Because I believe I have been so ignorantly blinded by the devil concerning masturbation. It seems as though everyone is asking whether it is wrong. In my opinion, it is. I've read every book on the market concerning this, I've sat in on counseling sessions, I've read the Word of God and prayed, and this is what the Lord has shown me.

But how does one stop doing these things? For me masturbation is a real problem. I've done it for the past eight years. If I didn't do it one time a day I would do it two or three times a day, even more. I feel completely helpless in this area because I feel it has become an obsession that I believe God wants me to stop. Therefore the spiritual me says, "Stop it." But then there's the flesh that says, "But it feels so good." Although I've known the Lord for eight years I don't have the willpower to stop masturbating. What do I do? As I've said previously, I've been counseled, read books and other materials, especially the Bible, I've been prayed for by others and myself. Nothing has worked. What do I do?

A: I'm afraid I haven't found a secret to controlling masturbation that others have overlooked. If you've been counseled and prayed for and you've studied the Bible, you've probably soaked up most of the Bible's wisdom on this subject.

Still, I'd like to mention several things that I think are crucial in winning any battle with sin.

The first is soaking in forgiveness. Sometimes we think that if we threaten ourselves, pretending that God will hate us if we fail, we'll put enough pressure on ourselves to make us stop. It never works for long. By punishing ourselves we really cut ourselves off from God's love and from the joyful, peaceful reassurance we ought to enjoy as Christians. It's God's love that gives us power to overcome evil, not threats of punishment. When you realize how much God loves you, you want to follow what he says, and his life in you gives you the power to obey.

Second, don't go it alone. Instead of asking someone to counsel and pray for you once, ask someone to counsel and pray with you every day or every week. The steady encouragement of another Christian will keep you from the drastic ups and downs that often make you mess up.

Third, don't play all or nothing. Don't let one failure add up to total failure. If you cut your failures in half, that's real progress, praise God! Be willing to settle for progress in your battle.

Personally, I have not been able to eliminate all envy and malice in my thoughts. Occasionally I find myself envious of another person and have to ask for God's forgiveness and help. But that doesn't mean I see my life as total failure. I am less envious than I used to be. I am going the direction God wants me to go, and for that I'm thankful.

Sometimes we all need to face the fact that you don't get to heaven while living on earth. We aren't perfect, and our lives aren't pure joy. The whole earth, Paul says in Romans 8, is groaning the painful groans of childbirth, waiting for something better! It can seem like a long wait. What's crucial is that we remember what the final goal is. We'll someday be with God, and he will make up for everything we have missed. Our struggles and pain, even dealing with temptation, are struggles toward that happiness. Yet the happiness is already sure, because Jesus has triumphed over evil completely. You will get there, in God's arms. For now, keep on growing and trying and struggling. But be sure you never lose the ultimate security: the wonderful fact that since God is for you, no one and nothing can ultimately stand against you. Nothing—not even your own weakness—can separate you from his love.

What about feelings of guilt, separation from God, and low self-esteem?

Q: I appreciate your words about masturbation. I have struggled with this over the years, and I still struggle with it. So I wanted to share some of the things I have learned.

As you have pointed out, masturbation is not really a moral issue. But the feelings of guilt, separation from God, and low self-esteem combine to turn the entire situation into a moral problem. While the act itself might not be wrong, the feelings that accompany it tend to create a chasm between ourselves and God. Although the chasm may not exist from God's point of view, it can be very real and damaging to our Christian walk.

I have wondered whether this lack of self-control makes me unworthy of the Christian service I am involved in, if my work is just a farce, meaningless because of this rotten spot in my life. I think Satan capitalized on my ignorance and for a number of years minimized my Christian witness because I didn't believe in myself.

I don't think the issue of masturbation will decide our eternal home, but I think it can be very damaging. It can become a controlling habit that demoralizes and ruins self-esteem. Instead of continuing to practice it, hoping the desire will eventually fade away, we need to face it straight on. We need to realize that it is not sin but can be harmful. We must not let feelings of guilt cause us to become passive, afraid to serve God because of our "unworthiness."

I still masturbate occasionally, but have learned some things and am still learning. Since I couldn't quit, I decided to cut down. I either limit myself each week or set dates and don't masturbate before that prearranged day. This helps me feel more in control and has given me a better self-image. At least I am trying.

I've discovered that once I entertain the thought in my mind, even to argue against it, I've lost the battle. Satan doesn't tempt me simply because he wants me to sin, but because he wants to defeat my usefulness as a Christian through feelings of guilt.

So when the desire arises, I immediately tell myself no and claim victory through Jesus over the temptation. It works pretty well, but not all the time. I do give in occasionally, and I'm learning to deal with myself when I do. I have to remind myself that I must not let Satan bind me with guilt. Jesus forgives sin and he can forgive this.

A: Thanks for telling your story so frankly. It sounds as though you've found a good balance for yourself. Whatever we say about masturbation, we can't question that the guilt it brings can be destructive.

Recently I was talking with a youth pastor who said, "I don't believe the action is what's wrong; the 'thought life' is the problem." I agree with him. However, "thought life" covers more than sexual fantasies. It covers those lies that latch onto masturbation: "I'm worthless. I'm a hopeless sinner. I'm filthy. God can never accept me." Most people who masturbate will continue masturbating, no matter how they feel about it. If there is a secret technique that will guarantee quitting, I don't know it yet. But that doesn't mean individuals are helpless to do anything about it.

Setting realistic goals and keeping them will help you cope with the sense of worthlessness and guilt. Controlling your erotic fantasies, making sure you stay away from pornography, learning to look at girls with a grateful, appreciative eye for the person you see rather than the body alone—these can help change your whole focus of thought. Positive friendships may replace the loneliness often at the root of compulsive masturbation. Most important, I think, learning to appreciate the full, warm forgiveness of God, who has not even thought your problem significant enough to warn against it in the Bible, can help you eliminate the "thought life" of worthlessness. You seem to have fought through the worst of these problems in a very positive way. I hope your example will encourage others.

7. *Homosexuality*

What does God think about homosexuality, and how can I deal with my homosexual feelings in light of this?

Q: I am gay. Or at least bisexual. I am also a Christian. I have been a Christian for four years. Most people's response to these facts is, "Well, if you made a true commitment, you wouldn't struggle with this." Or, "You can't be a Christian and be gay too." So I am a poor excuse for a Christian. I know what I do is wrong, but I still go on and do it. That is why I am writing to you. *What is wrong with me?* Do I need psychological help? Are you going to give me the "Jesus is the true answer" bit? (Though I know he is.) I just can't do it alone. I don't even know if I want to change. What should I do?

A: Let me start with your comment that you are a poor excuse for a Christian. There, at least, we are on common ground. I am a poor excuse for a Christian. We all are, if I read my Bible correctly. Nobody deserves to be treated lovingly by God; we all act in ways that would justify his turning away from us. Recognizing our total lack of credibility before him is a necessary starting point for grasping his attitude toward us. Because instead of turning from us, God welcomes us into his family and calls us his children.

God does not stop there, however. Any loving father trains his children, wanting them to grow up healthy. For your own good, God has expressed his expectations regarding your choices. He is not ambiguous. God does not want you living a gay lifestyle.

The Bible considers homosexual actions wrong. There isn't a great deal of material dealing with it; in the Old Testament it simply is declared off-limits, and that is carried over in the New Testament. The only passage that gives a hint of why it is wrong is Romans 1:26–27. There Paul discusses homosexuality in the context of people that have turned their back on God and have succeeded in twisting far away from what is "natural." Paul probably was thinking of the story of creation in Genesis, where it is said that God made man in his own image "male and female." We're sexual people—that's what's "natural"—and sex was made to be between male and female. We learn something about ourselves and about God through the wonderful erotic attraction and interaction of male and female. We learn even if we never marry, for we take part in those interactions at other levels.

That is the basic threat—that you would lose out on part of your identity. Your true identity in Christ isn't homosexual. Some experts say nearly everyone has homosexual desires to some extent. But the sexual focus of our lives is meant to be the opposite sex, for that is how we discover more about ourselves.

It is important to distinguish between your personality structure and the way you live it out. In other words, there is a difference between homosexual tendencies and a homosexual lifestyle. Everyone has certain dispositions that lead to particular strengths and weaknesses. The Big Lie of the sexual-freedom revolution is that you have to follow your sexual preference (whatever it is), that you have no choice. If I fall in love with someone, it's inevitable we'll end up in bed— unless I am a repressed and unhappy individual determined to stay in an unhappy marriage. If you feel attracted to other men, you will either "stay in the closet," repressed and unhappy, or you will enter the free-flowering splendor of the gay community.

But this is sheer nonsense. It's really just a variation on the old line a guy gives who wants to take a girl to bed: "Fate meant us to be together. It's bigger than both of us. It's chemistry." One difference between human beings and animals is that we can control our sexuality; it doesn't have to control us. If we all did everything we felt like doing, the world would be sheer chaos. Instead, as rational, thinking creatures, we take our many desires into consideration—desires for sexual release, for personal intimacy, for long-lasting friendships, for marriage and children, for many things—and we decide on a course. We choose a lifestyle that really suits us. We may need to say no to certain desires, but the overall result will be positive, fitting our personal needs.

Scripture does not indicate that it is wrong to be tempted. In fact, temptations are normal. The fact that you are tempted to have sexual relations with other men may reflect badly on our sex-crazed society, which inflames our tendencies, or it may reflect badly on your family background, as some psychologists say. I don't see that it reflects badly on you. How you came by the desires that trouble you I do not know. I suspect that most people feel a certain amount of sexual ambiguity, some people more than others.

I get many letters from young people who are afraid they are homosexuals. They've never lived a gay lifestyle, but they feel some variance in their sexual longings—maybe the opposite sex does not attract them in the way they expect is normal, or maybe they have tender feelings for a friend of the same sex. The gay movement claims that one out of ten people is a homosexual and that if you are one you can't do a thing about it. So the question arises: "Am I one?" Once the idea is planted, it tends to grow. And if a person tries it out, he will probably find that, indeed, he can be sexually aroused by his own sex. Therefore, he thinks, he must be gay. In reality, he may merely be ambivalent. In another society, in another time, he would have channeled his sexual desires in a different direction. Sexuality is more fluid than the gay movement leads people to believe. Sexual attraction is as much mental as physical.

You cannot choose your desires, but you can choose your lifestyle. As you say, your feelings and desires for sex will still be there. But what does that prove? Mine are still there too, but I have chosen to focus them within the marriage relationship. That means saying yes to some desires and no to a great many others. Some Christians are single, and they live with continuing heterosexual or homosexual desires. Need they be unhappy? The Bible answers a resounding no! The single, celibate life is honored in the New Testament without reservation. Everyone is called to it for some portion of his or her life. Some are called to it permanently. Jesus was, Paul possibly was, and countless other great and inspiring Christians through the ages have been celibate. Jesus' words in Matthew 19:12 suggest that the call to singleness is not always based on great religious feeling. Practical factors enter: "For some are eunuchs because they were born that way; others were made that way by men; and others have renounced marriage because of the kingdom of heaven." All three causes are honorable.

I believe singleness is the healthy and blessed lifestyle for you at this point. It won't be sheer bliss—I don't know of any lifestyle that is, realistically. And because your struggles are less acceptable in our society than mine, you will suffer a special loneliness in them. Given the judgmental disgust that many people feel regarding homosexuality, you can't expect the sympathies of vast numbers of people. However, you can hope to find the help and support of some.

Don't exaggerate the difficulty of sharing your situation privately with concerned, caring Christians. Many will not be able to accept and understand your situation, but many others will. I know some Christians who would be delighted to commit themselves to regular prayer and encouragement for someone in your shoes.

You cannot change your lifestyle alone. That is why I strongly encourage you to begin today asking God to put before you one or more people whom you can confide in with complete confidence. You need them not just to listen to you and accept you, but to play an active, caring part in your life, meeting regularly with you for prayer and Bible study. You need to take the risk of revealing your inner thoughts so that you can quit living in lonely secretiveness and begin to develop satisfying, deep relationships. Jesus is the answer to all our problems, but he doesn't work in a purely spiritual way. He has a physical and relational reality, what the Bible calls "the body of Christ"—that is, the church.

I look for the day when Christians will get over their homophobia and realize that those with homosexual temptations differ very little from the rest of us. We all struggle with temptations, and the Bible never treats one sin as worse than another. In the fellowship of the Holy Spirit, which is the togetherness binding Christians, we come closest to grasping Christ's full and final victory over sin.

There is no mysterious, awesome power in homosexual temptations. Temptation is temptation—we all know how impossible it can be when we are in the wrong situation and how easy to resist when we leave that situation. You say you are not sure that you want to change. I think you do want to change, but you are not sure you can. The gay movement says that you cannot, that you can only repress your natural feelings. That is not so. It is most natural to follow Jesus. You were made to do that.

What about homosexual marriage?

Q: I agree that to be a Christian, a person should want to save his body for just one person with whom he will spend and share the rest of life. If a Christian who is homosexual maintains this stand, then what is wrong with his or her being gay? Where does the Bible say it is wrong?

A: The Bible doesn't address the concept of homosexual marriage; it simply says that homosexuality is wrong. In the Old Testament homosexual acts were treated extremely seriously, and the New Testament carries this attitude on. You can find the subject treated in Romans 1:26–27; 1 Corinthians 6:9; and 1 Timothy 1:10. The Bible doesn't really discuss why it's wrong, or under what conditions; it just says it's wrong. Homosexuality was a common fact of Greek life, thoroughly accepted. So the Bible was, even then, swimming against the tide in condemning it.

The same is true for the Bible's condemnation of all extramarital sex. In both Old and New Testament times, many people were very open to all kinds of sex. The Jews and the Christians stood out because they weren't.

The reason goes back to Genesis 2 where God made Adam and Eve intimate partners for life. He created them male and female because male alone—Adam's situation before Eve—was "not good." The loving complementarity of two *different* sexes is very important, according to the Bible. Homosexual sex, like extramarital sex, is wrong because it is contrary to his will and is far less than the best—and God means "the best" to be the only experience for his people.

Can a homosexual change and develop heterosexual feelings?

Q: I live constantly wishing I could bring my problem out in the open so I could get help. I also live constantly in fear that somehow my deep secret (which I've told only one person) will be exposed and then I'll be rejected. My secret is, I think I'm a homosexual.

I guess I had a pretty average upbringing. Emotions were not really encouraged in my family, so we weren't very close. When I hit my teenage years I found out that I enjoyed the arts, such as drama, writing, and music, though guys are supposed to enjoy sciences. I began to feel I was different.

Instead of the usual adolescent fantasies about girls, I had them about other guys—first my friends at school, and then other men in magazines. When I was fourteen I made friends with a twenty-one-year-old guy called Kevin. He was a great friend and a strong Christian. I became dependent on him. He was like an older brother I'd never had. But soon I started to fantasize about having a physical relationship with him. To try to prove to myself that I was masculine (and to prove it to others, too) I got a girlfriend who loved me a lot. We would get physical but I could never reach a climax. This whole time I was going to church, and I knew I was a Christian.

At sixteen I got involved with a guy a year and a half younger whom I was baby-sitting. It was purely physical. We didn't care for each other much at all. At the same time I was still having sex with my girlfriend. Because I was scared of everything that was going on, when I hit seventeen I went far away to college. I was also having home problems—I couldn't get along with any of my family.

I came to my Christian college planning on starting anew. At first things went fine. I got involved in a college singing group. My grades were good. But then last semester I was talking to a friend of my ex-roommate, and suddenly he touched me. I thought that I had gotten away from that but immediately I felt the old excitement come back. We became physically involved. Afterwards I felt nothing but hate for this guy. Cheap and dirty! To this day I won't talk to him or even look his way.

At Christmas I took the train to visit my uncle. When I got there, I got to know the girl next door, and we ended up having sex. (Making love is not the truth—it was just sex.) I was trying again to prove that I am a man. On the way back on the train I met a guy who was gay, and I talked to him hoping he could help me. He acted as if he really cared for me. So we had sex. After that I never heard from him or saw him again. I know it's so wrong. I wish I didn't have these feelings. I often ask God, why me? Help me!

There is honestly no one I know whom I could talk to, but I feel like I'm a hypocrite, leading a double life. I want to be normal, but I want to be loved. Please help—you're my last chance.

A: My heart goes out to you. Not only are you stuck—like many people—in a rut of sexual behavior you can't seem to control. But your sexual ambiguity makes you question your very status as a man.

The first thing I want to say is that your manhood can't be proved by having sex with girls, or disproved by your interest in other men. You're a man because God made you a man. Your identity comes from him. Sexual labels, I'm convinced, do no good and much harm. For reasons that aren't fully understood, some people feel attracted to others of their own sex. But that doesn't make you "homosexual," as though you were a different species. It only makes you a human being who must, like all human beings, deal with desires and attractions that lead in the wrong direction. So don't label yourself, and don't let anyone else label you. If you use any label, call yourself simply a child of God.

The second thing I want to tell you is that repressing your feelings won't make them go away. Running away won't help either. It's more likely to intensify your feelings—they grow in the dark. All this secretive, neurotic testing of your sexuality has the effect of estranging you from yourself and from others. What you want and need—as all of us do—is to love and be loved. Your experiments, with men and with women, only make you more desperately in need of love and less likely to find it. You don't need to "prove" that you're a man. (There's no way to prove it, anyway.) What you need is loving, open, nurturing relationships, in which you can face your problems.

You need, therefore, to come out of the closet. I don't by that mean declaring your homosexuality. I've already said that labels don't help; they confuse. But you do need to stop being secretive about your struggles. You do need to share with some key people who will help you, encourage you, and pray for you as a normal human being.

Unfortunately, not everyone will be able to do that. Some people really are terribly frightened by homosexual behavior. However, I believe many if not most mature Christians are anxious to help someone like you, and not to condemn. I'd urge you to take some risks and go looking for such people.

Recently I spent considerable time with leaders of Exodus International, a coalition of Christian ministries that help those struggling as you are. I came away with a renewed sense of hope. The men and women I met weren't gay-bashers. Neither were they fanatics, out of touch with reality. They seemed very down-to-earth. They had a good sense of humor. They emphasized that there is no overnight change of sexual identity, but they also emphasized that deep change is possible. Most of them had gone through such a change themselves. Many were happily married. Their own lives and testimonies were a strong indication of what can happen for people who are committed to following Christ and receiving help from other Christians.

Exodus International publishes a list of member organizations. You can find them throughout the nation and in some other countries. Exodus also has some helpful publications. You can write to them at P.O. Box 2121, San Rafael, California 94912. I'd recommend that you do so.

You may be encouraged by a letter I received from someone who is successfully coping with feelings like your own:

> I recently picked up a copy of *Campus Life*. It's been several years since I last followed the magazine, and

your column "Love, Sex & the Whole Person." In this issue there was a letter from a guy struggling with homosexuality. Those letters always used to get me, since that was my background too.

During my early college years, your response to those guys (and girls) was the only source of understanding that I could find from Christian circles. It was reassuring for me to hear of other Christians in the same bondage of the heart that I was experiencing. You always claimed that a person doesn't have to stay homosexual and that Christ could begin a new work inside, which gave me hope. (Although how that was done was rather elusive to me.)

In the past four years I have discovered that there is a network of ministries across the U.S. that help those struggling with homosexuality. I immediately got involved in the local ministry and found that freedom is a reality. Of course there is no magic cure, apart from the restoring of my identity as a man and as a child of God.

After four years I can honestly say that homosexuality is no longer compulsive, and the intensity of it all has declined to where it's not much of an issue in my life any more. I don't think about looking at men, and in fact I have several good friendships with (straight) guys with no erotic overtones at all. There is still some temptation left, but nowhere close to what I felt before. Also now there is heterosexuality, where there was none before.

It hasn't been easy. It's been an intense struggle of facing some big deficits and the pain of how I see myself deep down. I found my homosexuality was really the desire to devour someone else's masculinity in order to feel secure in my own gender. The Lord asked me if I was willing to face the hurts and allow him to restore me. The outcome of doing this has been just incredible.

I wish that four years ago I could have read a letter from someone about their testimony of homosexuality. I wish I could have read that there were groups to help people like me. I want to thank you that back then you planted the seed of hope in my heart. God really does bring restoration for those he loves.

How should Christians respond to homosexuals?

Q: About last May I got to know another guy I'll call Roger. I was new in school, and he was friendly, plus we had a couple of classes together. Now I've found out there are lots of stories going around about his being a homosexual. The whole school seems to know about it, and people say if you hang around with him you must be a homosexual too. This was really a shock to me—I had no idea. It hurts me to think of forgetting Roger, because I like him and also I know that he is very lonely, and if I drop him as a friend that isn't going to help him any. I feel awkward around him now—if he really is a homosexual, I don't want to give him the wrong idea, and I don't want other people to get the wrong idea either. I never heard of anything like this before. What should I do?

A: First of all, I wouldn't jump to the conclusion that Roger is really a homosexual. People can be very cruel. In some schools, coaches and teachers associate certain kinds of behavior with masculinity. Any guy who's sensitive, who doesn't want to fight at the drop of a hat, who doesn't want to play contact sports, is labeled a homosexual. Sometimes the tag comes from subtler things than that: the way he walks or talks. Make sure you're not condoning other people's stereotypes by playing along.

Of course, there is also the possibility that Roger really has homosexual feelings. That would be no reason for deserting him as a friend. A homosexual hasn't chosen those feelings. He needs friendship and support, not ostracism. Regardless of the label's accuracy, you should stick with Roger as a friend. You can use some of your influence with other people to allow entrance for Roger, so that he can become less isolated in his loneliness.

That may cost something in terms of your own social

success. You may remember that Jesus had the same kind of a problem, though with a different cast. People complained that Jesus hung around with sinners, drinkers, and thieves. Jesus reminded his critics that people who have everything together really don't need him. Only sick people need a doctor.

I'd suggest you talk to Roger about the rumors. I'm sure he knows about them. It will probably help your friendship to bring them out in the open, especially if you can convey that you are his friend no matter what. Maybe Roger can be honest with you about his problems, whatever they are, and you'll be able to help him or put him in touch with experienced counselors who can.

My sister is a homosexual. How can I talk with her?

Q: I read a letter from a homosexual who is a Christian, and now I can understand my sister much better. She is a homosexual and, I believe, a Christian.

To me, homosexuality is no worse than any other habitual sin. I know that God disapproves—that is clear in Romans 1—but I believe any other sin is equally wrong.

Not to say that I approve of or accept homosexuality, because I do not, but it is very difficult for me to pray for my sister. How can I ask God to show her her faults and lead her back to him, when I'm no better than she is? I need as much guidance and direction as she does. I feel like I'm judging her by praying for her, and putting myself higher. But I know I'm no more Christian than she is. Am I wrong?

A: You're right, and you're wrong. It's true that all sins are equal in God's sight, and none of us can claim the least superiority to anyone else. Your sense that you are no better

than your sister is right. As Paul wrote in Galatians 6:3–4, "If anyone thinks he is something when he is nothing, he deceives himself. Each one should test his own actions. Then he can take pride in himself, without comparing himself to somebody else. . . ." Or, as Paul wrote to Corinth, "If you think you are standing firm, be careful that you don't fall!" (1 Corinthians 10:12).

But even though all sins are equal in God's sight, some sins do more earthly harm than others. Sexual sin often seems to do more harm than some other sins because it is so deeply personal, "closer" to us than anything else we do. "All other sins a man commits are outside his body, but he who sins sexually sins against his own body" (1 Corinthians 6:18). So I think you are perfectly realistic in focusing concern on your sister's sexual choices. They may be a keystone to a whole range of values she is choosing. This would be true whether she had heterosexual or homosexual temptations.

Where do you get this idea that you can't show concern for your sister without acting superior to her? True, some people focus exclusively on others' shortcomings, as though they had none of their own. Jesus warned such people, "First take the plank out of your own eye, and then you will see clearly to remove the speck from your brother's eye" (Matthew 7:5). But when you realize how needy you are yourself, and how much Christ has forgiven you, you ought much more to want your sister to find the same help. Does not one beggar guide another to the place where they are handing out bread?

However, you should do it gently, with great care. In the same passage in which Paul tells us not to compare ourselves with others, he gives this recipe: "Brothers, if someone is caught in a sin, you who are spiritual should restore him gently. But watch yourself, or you also may be tempted. Carry each other's burdens, and in this way you will fulfill the law of Christ" (Galatians 6:1–2).

The law of Christ is that you must love your neighbor as yourself. Love is not, as many people in our time assert, approving anything anyone does. It is recognizing sin as a

crushing burden and helping to carry the load. Praying for your sister is a good place to start. And perhaps, since you also carry burdens, you could ask her to pray for you.

Why should I be condemned to celibacy because of a condition I didn't choose?

Q: I cannot even begin to comprehend your views on homosexuality. You seem to believe that because you are heterosexual, you are able to lead a "normal" life. By "normal" I mean being allowed by society to date, fall in love, and marry. I, on the other hand, because I am gay, must through no choice of my own either lead a celibate life or be forced into a marriage with a woman I could not possibly keep happy or be happy with.

I believe you cannot possibly give an unbiased view on homosexuality because you seem to already have your ideas set in your head and because you do not understand homosexuals, nor do you wish to. I also believe you have quite a prejudice against gay people because of your passing judgment—something that, as a Christian, you are taught is only for the Lord to do.

I believe that the Lord made me the way I am for a reason, although I do not know what that reason is. I have tried for years to fight my feelings due to the viewpoints of people such as you. These struggles have resulted in three separate suicide attempts. I have finally accepted myself as I am and have realized that I cannot change myself. I have never been happier!

Because I am gay, that does not mean I have no morals. That is another misconception you seem to have. Although I

have been sexually active in the past, I have resolved to save myself for the person I will spend the rest of my life with.

Thank you for your time in reading this. I'm sure it will have no effect on your views, but maybe it can change the minds of other people and help gay Christians who read your column.

A: Thank you for writing. It's obvious that I haven't been communicating very well what I believe. I welcome a chance to say it more clearly.

I don't know that I can claim to fully understand homosexuals, or heterosexuals for that matter. I don't fully understand myself. But I do understand that to grow up with strong homosexual feelings is very difficult and often induces self-hatred and doubt. I understand that the gay liberation movement gives many such people a sense of liberty after years of hiding and self-hate. I understand that many homosexuals inside and outside the gay movement are fine, moral, compassionate people.

I don't doubt that you are unable to change yourself. If there is any hope for change, it is in Christ's power, not the homosexual's. I do know of many people who lived as homosexuals for years and were able through the power of Christ to convincingly shift direction. I am also aware that many homosexuals doubt the reality of the changes in these people's lives.

God, I am sure, is able to change a homosexual's orientation, or any other orientation. I have little doubt that he sometimes does so. However, I know the power of sexual patterns, and I know there is no automatic, magical way to change them. They usually change, if they change at all, through long, determined struggle and a lot of outside help. You don't ordinarily change your sexual patterns, heterosexual or homosexual, by praying alone in your room.

I doubt that we dramatically disagree in these areas. Yet there are two areas where we do disagree. One is about celibacy. You seem to think of it as a punishment—a curse of abnormality and deprivation. I can understand that view: most people in America think of it that way. But Christians have never thought of it that way. They have, since the time of Jesus, thought of it as a privilege and an opportunity to serve God. If Jesus was celibate and Paul was celibate, it was obviously a good condition. I don't see that a person's free choice has anything to do with it, either. Paul calls singleness a gift in 1 Corinthians 7—a gift from God. God chooses what gifts to give his people. Our choice is how we receive and use those gifts.

I was celibate for twenty-seven years, and I regard those as wonderful, full, rich years. I do not regret them, nor do they make me feel sorry for my friends who are celibate now. These friends miss some great joys in not being married, but they can gain others. For me to say to someone who is homosexual, "You should follow Christ and be celibate," is not offering a message of judgment but of hope. I would say exactly the same thing to an unmarried heterosexual. (I would never, under any circumstances, urge someone to marry a person with whom he or she could never be happy. Just the opposite.)

One principal reason why I see celibacy as a gift to homosexuals is that I think promiscuity is a source of deep unhappiness, to them and to anyone else. The gay movement is highly promiscuous, as you know. Even now, while AIDS rages, surveys show that the average homosexual has several different partners per month. They risk their lives to do so. I don't understand why they do, but I wonder if there is something inherently unstable about homosexual relationships. Perhaps this is one reason why the Bible encourages people to leave them rather than try to make permanent relationships with them in a "homosexual marriage." The Bible regards all homosexual relationships (not persons) as being far from what God wants his people to enjoy.

I don't know why you are oriented the way you are. I believe, however, that God created you and intends good for your life. I am glad you are no longer sexually promiscuous.

But you could do much better by putting your life into God's hands and asking him what he made you for. I believe he made you to serve him, and to obey him, and to be happy in a celibate condition.

8. Singleness

Can I really be happy if I never marry?

Q: Although I have been reading your column for nearly ten years, I have just now gotten the courage to write concerning a problem that literally dominates my mind. To put it simply, I don't get dates. It's a mystery to me and to a lot of other people. I just seem unable to put my finger on the reason.

I am not bad-looking. I am intelligent. People tell me I have a wonderful personality, and I try to be friendly to everyone. Still, no one asks me out. I've got to say that at age twenty-two this problem is nearly tearing me up. I have tried giving up on men altogether, but it doesn't work. I am so lonely. All my friends have boyfriends or are married.

Please do not assume that I have no male friends. In fact, my best friends are male. (This has not always been the case.) I am a Christian, and I know of other pretty and friendly Christian girls in the same situation. What is the problem? I have a lot of love that I'd like to share with someone. I hope it isn't going to be wasted.

I have thought that maybe God wants me to be single. However, I also believe that he wants to give me the desires of my heart, and frankly, the idea of singleness is one that I would find most difficult to accept.

I've prayed extensively about this and am trying to "keep the faith," but my tough outer layer is growing thin. I feel that I've missed out on so much already. I've lost nearly all my self-confidence.

A: You're right in believing that God wants to give you the desires of your heart, but you're misunderstanding the implications of that. Very few of us start out wanting exactly what's best for us. If what we wanted *were* the best for us, God would be in the business of giving out candy, sex, hot cars, popularity, and movie contracts. He's not. So God often has to change the desires of our hearts in order to fulfill them. If he wants you to be single (and he obviously does right now), he also wants to get you to the place where you're happy with it.

You don't have to become delighted with the idea that you'll be single for the rest of your life. Tomorrow will take care of itself. Today is where God wants to affect your thinking. Today, in the situation where he has put you, he wants you to find purpose and joy. He'll help you with that.

You say you've prayed extensively about your single status. I'd encourage you to start praying that you'll make the most of each single day. You say you have a lot of love to share that you hope isn't going to be wasted. My question is: Will it be wasted today? I'm quite sure there are people around you who need your love. Maybe sharing with them isn't the desire of your heart. Maybe you want to share your love only with a boyfriend. If so, God will need to change your heart so that you can develop a new attitude.

Singleness can be good. It was for Jesus. If this is what God wants you to experience, he'll make it good, hard as it may be for you to imagine that.

That isn't the message coming through our society (or our churches). Our world has put sex on a very high pedestal—and along with it marriage or living-together relationships. In today's society never to make love, never to share the deepest personal intimacies with another person, seems synonymous with being undesirable and possibly even perverted. I think it's largely this image that has made so many single people so unhappy. Being single isn't bad in itself, but if negative attitudes dominate your mind, you'll be miserable.

It is possible that God may want you to be single. He wants everyone to be single for at least a part of life. The Bible doesn't talk about singleness as second-rate. In fact, it speaks of it positively. In the Middle Ages Christians took this so far as to regard marriage as second-rate. We seem to have swung the other way now and need to get a balanced view. Both marriage and singleness are gifts from God.

Ponder for a minute one fact: Jesus Christ, our Lord, never married. He never had sexual intercourse. Yet he was perfect, and perfectly fulfilled. He lived the kind of life we want to imitate. That doesn't mean that all of us ought to want to be single; there's no doubt that marriage is the best way for most men and women. But it should say one thing for certain: singleness need not be second-rate. It need not be unfulfilled. It need not be unhappy.

Paul wasn't married either, at least at the height of his career. He recommended the single life in 1 Corinthians 7, calling it a gift. (Strange that this is the one gift most people would prefer to exchange.) And Jesus himself, in Matthew 19:10–12, talks positively about the reasons some people should remain unmarried.

Some people, of course, try to peer into the future and find out whether God has given them the gift of singleness. They want to know, I guess, whether someday God is going to award them a spouse, or whether they should forget about relating to the opposite sex, shrug their shoulders, and settle down to the long grind. Maybe God does actually tell some people ahead of time whether they will or won't be married, but most of us seem to find out what he wants one day at a time. I have no reason to believe that a "gift" of singleness can't be temporary. God may completely fulfill you as a single person at one stage of life, but at another he may call you to marriage. By the same token, a married person never knows when his spouse's death might call him back to the "gift" of singleness.

One of the saddest things I see, then, is the tendency for single people to live life as though waiting for something or someone to happen to them. They act as though they are in limbo, waiting to become capable of life when the magic day at the altar comes. Of course, they're usually disappointed. In some cases they become such poor specimens of humanity that no one wants to marry them. More often they do get married, only to discover that they haven't received the key to life; the initiative and character they should have developed before marriage is exactly what they need *in* marriage. And they are still lonely and frustrated.

What do you do with a gift? You open it. You admire it. You thank the giver. You use it. And this is what you ought to do with the singleness God has called you to for the present.

Is it worth waiting for "the right one"?

Q: In answer to a recent letter, you stated that sometimes nice guys seem scarce, but eventually, if you wait, they'll find you.

Well, I'm still waiting. I'm twenty-three. I've dated many guys and not one has appreciated my abstinence from sex.

I met a twenty-seven-year-old guy a few weeks ago, and he asked me out. Two dates later he had me convinced he respected my standards, that he liked me, and that he'd be seeing me a lot. That was the last time he called.

The guy I loved in high school and early college married someone else, as did a man I fell for last year. People tell me to wait, that God has someone special for me. But in the meantime I feel hurt, lonely, and used. Any word of encouragement?

$A:$ Your letter reminded me of a conversation I had with a friend a few years ago. We were sitting where we could see our wives walking and talking together. He said to me, with a very happy grin, "I think it was worth waiting, don't you?"

My wife and I were married when we were twenty-seven. As I rounded twenty-four, twenty-five, and twenty-six, I had severe doubts that I would ever marry. But looking back, I wouldn't want to have married a moment sooner. Really, twenty-three is rather early for you to start despairing. I have friends, both men and women, who married for the first time—and very happily!—when they were in their forties.

People find it difficult to remember that they'll marry only one person. It doesn't matter whether you have scores of men hanging around. You don't need scores. You require only one—the right one.

There is no guarantee, of course, that you will ever marry. But if you don't, it won't be because God was unable to deliver the goods. The logistics of creating the right number of men and women and getting them to the right places at the right time are, I assume, not difficult for a God who made heaven and earth. If you remain sensitive to God's leading and you don't marry, it will be because he has a better plan more suited to you. I realize that this is theoretical, whereas the lack of male companions is very real to you right now. But reading the Bible, you will repeatedly find this message: what meets the eye is not necessarily the truth. We are to build our lives on what is invisible.

The worst mistake you could make now, at twenty-three, is to orient your whole life around "what guys want." This happens when people become desperate to marry, and it is usually transparent and repulsive to the opposite sex. You do not want to please "guys," you want to please one guy whom you don't know anything about yet. The safest plan is to orient your life around God and his plans and seek ways to enjoy your life now, the way it is. If you feel hurt, lonely, or used, you may be making yourself that way—by feeling sorry for yourself, by not taking opportunities to make nonromantic friends, and by not setting out to "use" your own life in a definite and useful way.

Look, I know it's not easy. But, believe me, being married is not easy either. I know plenty of married people who wish they were single! For all people, single or married, the rules are the same:

1. Be thankful for who you are and where you are.

2. Determine to make your life worthwhile to God, in attitude and in act.

3. Concentrate on loving your neighbor as much as you love yourself.

People who follow these rules are invariably people whom others admire. They are usually happy, too—most of the time.

9. *Marriage*

What makes a Christian marriage different?

Q: I'm dating a guy I've known for almost a year. He's all I've ever wanted and needed in a guy. He's good-looking, he cares about me, and above all he loves Jesus more than anything else. My problem is not sex, but more an understanding of what marriage and sex are all about. My boyfriend has really sparked my thought on this.

In a recent issue you wrote, "I suspect most people who have waited until marriage for sex did so with no understanding of what a Christian marriage is." Count me in. Just what is a Christian marriage? Is it being born again in Jesus and remaining pure until after the ceremony? It seems there should be so much more to it than that. Do I have my hopes way too high? What happens after that most important commitment? Life certainly must change for both people. Is the adjustment hard? And is that adjustment the foundation for a good future together?

I want more than anything to have a Christian marriage perfect in God's eyes. But no one's ever told me just exactly what that is.

A: It's sad no one has told you, because marriage is meant to be much more than a safe, legal place to have sex. You don't have your hopes set too high. Marriage is meant to be wonderful. God designed it to cure human loneliness. He

173

intended it to show the same kind of loving that Jesus shows for his people.

Yet it's hard to generalize about marriage, because marriage is the coming together of two unique people. That makes each marriage doubly unique. One couple will tell you the first year of marriage is the hardest. Another couple will sigh and say they had sheer bliss that first year, and it's been a muddy road ever since. I have friends who should get a combat medal for marriage, it's been so hard. Others just glide along, never fighting.

Still, there are some things that every Christian marriage should be and can be.

In a Christian marriage the husband and wife should be totally faithful. Usually this idea is put negatively—a Christian shouldn't fool around before the wedding and he doesn't fool around afterwards. But it's so much more than that. It means this: here is one person I can totally trust. He or she will not treat me unfairly. He'll be thinking of my best interests, caring for me, protecting me. I can let him know my deepest thoughts, let him see and know my body, let him experience my silly moods and my serious moods, knowing I won't be betrayed. Of course, the same faithfulness I get, I must be prepared to give—and then some.

Where there's faithfulness, there's the possibility of the deepest love. You can't love totally when the person you love may turn on you tomorrow. You can't tell secrets to someone who may leave next year. In a Christian marriage, this should never be a problem.

A Christian marriage should be a totally loving one. Love is a feeling, but as Walter Trobisch has put it in one of his books, it is a feeling to be learned. You have to nurture the feelings through action. You sacrifice for each other; you think of each other first. Every day when I go home, when I'm about five minutes away from seeing my wife, Popie, I try to start thinking about her and what her day may have been like. I ask God to help me respond to her in a way that's really loving. That's a small way of preparing for what I hope my whole attitude of love can become—not being wrapped up in my own feelings but concentrating on her and serving her.

In a Christian marriage the husband and wife should be a team, working together. You may love each other madly, but do you offer the world more as a couple than you would apart? This is another way of saying that Christian marriage is based on God's will, not just your own desires. It's not just to make you happy, but to make you a better Christian. Christian couples try to please each other, but they can't build their life on that pleasure principle. They also ask, "What can we do to serve God?" Even having children fits into this; you serve the children—and discipline them—because you believe God gave you that responsibility, not just because you "like kids."

Having said that, I should also say that a Christian marriage is sometimes imperfect. At least, all the ones I know about are. What makes a marriage Christian isn't that it's happier and healthier than others—though I think that most of the time it will be—but that the partners are trying to do greater things. They're not married just because it's convenient, or because they like each other's looks or personality, or because they feel tremendously in love, or because society expects them to get married, or for any number of other, typical reasons why people marry. Such reasons may have been the spark that got them started, but if they're trying to create a relationship that can in a small way show God's love to the world, they'll go beyond that spark. Christian marriage takes work. It also takes forgiveness when one or the other (or both) fails.

The final characteristic of a Christian marriage is the partners' submission to God's will. Sometimes that will be very difficult. Sometimes it will lead them in a direction that seems likely to make them unhappy. Sometimes it may put their careers or even their lives in danger. But a Christian marriage is one that belongs to Christ and in which the husband and wife consciously seek to find out what Christ wants to do with his possession.

How important are feelings in a marriage decision?

Q: I am twenty-two years old and have had my share of relationships. The person I'm dating now is the best yet. He's the most mature guy I've dated. He has his "act together" and gets along better with my family than any previous boyfriend. The latter is important because my folks are strong Christians and have always had high ideals for me. He has asked me to marry him, but I have hesitated because it's a rather awesome thing to consider spending the rest of your life with one person, and because I'm not sure of my love.

I realize there's no pat definition, but I'm confused as to love's relationship to "feelings." Although this boyfriend is probably "the best one" I've had yet, has many important qualities, is comfortable to be with, and gives me no reason for complaint, I don't really have any "warm, gooey" feelings about him. I'm not infatuated with him.

I guess I'm afraid my love isn't strong enough to carry me through the rough times. I worry that I may get tired of or bored with him. A lifetime is a long and important thing.

So my question is, Just how important are feelings to a relationship? I have been infatuated over guys before. Are feelings something that may pass, or do they really help carry you over the rough spots?

A: I think that in our society, feelings are pretty important. In cultures where marriages are arranged, less emotional love is usually expected between the partners. But in our culture, when we marry we demand intimacy, friendship, and romance. If you miss those in courtship, you may always miss them. Sometimes your emotions sense something that your mind can't define.

To some extent emotions do help you over rough spots in your marriage. They support your commitment. It is easier to act loving when you feel loving. And it is no struggle to stay faithful to someone you are crazy about.

But feelings have their limits, too. Without support, they will die out sooner or later. The qualities you admire in your friend—respect, maturity, compatibility—are essential to a good marriage, more essential than feelings. You can't do without them, no matter how much you love each other. Feelings and a solid relationship ought to go together.

Your lack of feelings isn't what bothers me the most. It's your motivation. I'm reading between the lines, but it sounds as though you think that because you are twenty-two it is "time" to marry. A better chance may not come along.

I do not consider this a good reason. The amount of "gooey feelings" may vary considerably with age and personality, and some people may marry, successfully, without any feeling of romance. But I believe any Christian must have a unique sense that this is the person and this is the time God has called the two together. A sense of God's guidance will help you through rough spots more than good feelings will.

You may still have doubts. I think everyone but a fool feels some doubt and fear. But you should be able to search your heart and say, in faith, that this person is the one in all the world God wants you to marry. That is a much more secure guideline than the feeling that he is probably "the best one" you've had yet.

You don't have to say no to him forever. But say no for now.

How do you know if this is "the right one"?

Q: My question is, How do you know when the right one has come along? Some say you can feel it, others say you cannot. So how does one come to know which person God plans for you to marry?

My boyfriend and I have been going together for almost three months now. We have a friendship that is both strong and Christ-centered. When I'm with him, I feel at total peace, like I could be with him always and never grow tired of having him around. We have many similar interests and with each passing day we find more things in common. Time is not a problem because we have the rest of our lives to live and be happy. We both agree we don't want to rush into anything. And yet, how does one know?

A: The answer I'm going to give you—I believe it's the Bible's—may frustrate you. You believe, and I do too, that there is a "right one" for you. God has someone particular in mind, assuming he wants you to marry at all. But how do you recognize this person when he comes along? How do you know for certain? The answer is, you don't know with absolute, final certainty until you find yourself at the front of the church, opening your mouth to say, "I do." Until that day you won't know for sure. After that day the issue is settled, forever.

I know that seems paradoxical. As is so often the case with the Bible, it doesn't solve your problem the way you wanted it solved. It seems like a trick. You want to know "the right one" in order to make the choice simple. Instead, the choice becomes more demanding. You make the choice on your own, and then when you've made it, you hear the door locking behind you. Your choice has suddenly become God's choice.

I believe we find this frustrating because we don't want to face the difficult facts about marriage—and ourselves. We want to reduce marriage mainly to a question of finding the right combination of personalities—like finding the right key for a lock. We hold potential partners up against a list of ideal qualities, to see how they rate.

I certainly believe that compatibility is important.

However, it is far from the most important criterion in a successful marriage. God's main focus is not compatibility, but a question that cuts to the heart of marriage: *Can you say, "I do" and stick with it until death?* If you can, then you have found "the right one"—and you have also become "the right one."

Do we see so much divorce, unhappiness, suicide, wife and child beating, and promiscuity because, through a mental mistake, millions of Americans found the "wrong person"? No. We want to blame our problems on "mistakes," preferably mistakes that no one could sensibly foresee. We want to do that because we can't bear to think of the alternative: that things go awry because we are wrong inside, because we can't take the pressures of life, and above all because we can't love and keep loving in the way that happy living demands.

God makes hard questions bore into you as you think about marriage. They are primarily questions about you, not your partner. Can you take the heat? Can you make the commitment and stick to it? God wants you to ask not only, "Is this the right person for me?" but "Am I the right person?" In his way of thinking, compatibility is always secondary to commitment.

From the day you make that commitment, your question about "the right person" is answered. He or she is the right person for you to stick to, love, and cherish. He or she may not prove to be the right person to make you happy, but he or she is certainly the right person to shape you—in better or worse conditions, in sickness or in health, in poverty or in wealth—into the person God wants you to become.

Although my answer is more than a little frustrating, it does respond to your questions. It says, first of all, that there is a right one for you, if you are called to marriage. This is more than saying that you have to make the best of a bad situation, or that divorce is never a good option for a Christian. It says that God himself puts his stamp of approval on your marriage. He says that the one you vow marriage to is his perfect will for your life—no ifs, ands, or buts. There is no such thing as second best in his thinking. There is no "might have been." He only urges you forward into the wonderful future he prepares for each of us. You can, therefore—in fact, you will—find "the right one." Every earnest Christian who marries will be married to the man or woman with whom God wants her or him to find marital fulfillment.

You even know how to find "the right one." You find him or her by marrying. You have a grave responsibility for making the choice. In making that choice, you are finding God's will.

Does this imply that you cannot make a mistake? Does it imply, in the extreme, that a Christian could marry a non-Christian, knowing full well that this violates 2 Corinthians 6:14, and yet find himself or herself perfectly within God's will? In one sense, no. Disobedience to God is always a mistake. It will get you loads of unhappiness and trouble.

And so will a marriage that is a "poor choice." If two people are incompatible, if one or both of them have extreme personality difficulties, if unhappy experiences with sexual abuse has made one or both of them unable to enjoy sexual contact, or if any one of a great number of problems pertains, the marriage will be difficult and, from one point of view, a "mistake."

Yet in another sense there are no mistakes. Because of his great love for marriage, God will take even these mistaken marriages for his own. This is Paul's explicit comment to the Corinthians, who wondered whether mixed marriages should be dissolved. (They had probably married when both were non-Christians, and later one of them had become converted.) Paul wrote, "If any brother has a wife who is not a believer and she is willing to live with him, he must not divorce her. And if a woman has a husband who is not a believer and he is willing to live with her, she must not divorce him. *For the unbelieving husband has been sanctified through his wife, and the unbelieving wife has been sanctified through her believing husband*" (1 Corinthians 7:12–14). The word *sanctified* means "made holy," or "set apart for God's work." Paul doesn't imply that non-Christians are automatically made into Christians through marriage. They are not. He doesn't imply that a Christian partner who disobeyed God would pay no penalty for his or her disobedience. He or she will pay a penalty. Paul does imply that God is willing to make a marriage into what it would not otherwise be: a vehicle for his best blessings to his people. For Paul, there is no hopeless marriage.

So may a Christian marry a non-Christian—or make some other unwise marriage plans? Not at all! How, in the first place, could a real Christian wish to disobey God and marry a non-Christian? Or why would a Christian want to enter marriage with unwise or hasty plans? For God has given marriage as a marvelous and wonderful gift. Marriage ought to be treated with reverent care, for that is how God treats it. Any other attitude can only lead you, and your partner, into the risk of great pain. Any other attitude would suggest that you are no more ready for marriage than a two-year-old is ready to defuse a delicate and complex time bomb.

Marriage should be entered into with reverent care. This is why you can legitimately hold a potential partner up to a list and see how he or she measures up. The proper purpose of the list—and I am going to give you a list in a moment—is to help you think about the commitment you are preparing to make. You want to be as sure as possible that you are making it wisely and will live with it happily, since marriage is not an experiment but an absolute commitment in God's sight. You want to be sure you can live with it and *want* to live with it. A list of qualities, properly used, helps you make that commitment with confidence and wisdom.

There is no perfect partner. You are not perfect, and neither will "the right one" be perfect. No matter whom you choose, you will have unhappy days. You want to make a wise decision, to find a partner who will give you joy and fellowship, whom you can join in serving God. You are looking for someone who fits you. You must test, and think, and pray, and talk, until conviction comes that you have found the person you want and need. Here are twenty questions that can help you think about "the right one."

1. *Can you talk?* Marriages aren't built on good looks but

on good communication. The most crucial question you can ask about a potential partner is, "Do we know how to communicate?"

2. *Can you play?* Life isn't all talk, either. A couple needs to be able to help each other relax, laugh, and have fun. If you can't do it, the heavy, heart-thumping seriousness of your love will wear out. Love without laughter is like bread without yeast: it doesn't rise.

3. *Can you work together?* Christian marriage is not merely an association for pleasure. It involves work. This comes naturally with living together. Somebody has to cook, clean, wash clothes, rake leaves. Eventually you will raise children. And a Christian marriage is meant to be a vehicle for God's love to the world. That takes work. So it's important that you work well together.

4. *Do you have mutual friends?* You aren't going to spend all your lives with just each other. You will need other friends, and it's important they not split you apart but bring you closer together.

5. *Are you proud of each other?* You need privacy to get acquainted, but fairly often couples in love become like a space satellite orbiting planet earth. They are in their own world. This is quite unrealistic. Marriage involves lots of others: friends, ex-boyfriends and ex-girlfriends, parents, pastors, neighbors, even enemies. You don't have to be intimate with all these. But you do need to be proud of your partner in their presence. A love that has no public strength is unlikely to endure.

6. *Are you intellectually on the same level?* Most of the time this goes with education. There are plenty of exceptions, but as a rule two people ought to have similar educational backgrounds.

7. *Do you have common interests?* Beyond "us" that is. Common interests are the raw material for friendship. If one person lives for sports, and the other grows nauseous at the sight of a football game, they will need to make major adjustments to each other.

The key word is "interest." You can cultivate an

interest. You can "take an interest" in a subject you never knew existed. You may not start out with much in common, but are you developing common interests?

8. *Do you share the same values*—about, for instance, being honest in "the little things" like income taxes? About the importance of a clean house and car? About the value of going to church every week? About the roles of men and women in marriage? About abortion? Divorce?

9. *Do you feel comfortable about how you make decisions together?* Most people assume a certain way to arrive at a decision—probably because their parents operated that way. Unhappiness comes when the husband and wife don't agree on the proper process.

10. *Do you help each other emotionally?* Everyone gets bruised and discouraged in the course of life. In good marriages, both partners draw encouragement and strength from each other. Your partner should be someone you go to for healing.

11. *Do you have absolute trust in each other?* Trust has to do with your assessment of a person's character. You trust someone if you have complete confidence that he or she will do what is right. If you lack trust, nothing can substitute for its absence. Complete trust in your partner's handling of money, drugs, and alcohol, and in his or her sexual fidelity, confidentiality, treatment of children, Christian faith, hard work, and truthfulness is essential. A lack of trust in any of these areas will do more than detract from your happiness. It will completely undermine it. You cannot do without trust.

12. *Are you more creative and energetic because of each other?* Some people say that love makes a person absentminded. It may do that at times. It may also make a person irritable, worried, or depressed—at times. Overall, though, love should give you both more life. Depression, worry, and lethargy are trouble signs. You shouldn't usually get less done because you're in love, but more. Love should make you more determined than ever to make the best of yourself and the work you do, because you want your partner to be proud of

you, and you feel responsible to him or her. You should bring out the best in each other.

13. *Do you help each other grow closer to God?* First and foremost, you both must have a relationship to God. This means more than having hung around a church. It means that you both talk to God, you listen to him, and you care about his Word. Good partners help each other grow in this relationship. A healthy relationship has a specifically spiritual dimension to it—it's not just assumed.

Second, at a purely practical level, you ought to be able to agree on a church to join. If you can't agree on a church, you're always going to be pulling in different directions, rather than pulling together.

Third, you ought to be at approximately the same level of Christian maturity. "Maturity" is hard to grade, but you know it when you see it. It's not intensity, but depth and consistency. Maturity comes as you learn to walk by the Spirit, and as the Spirit produces increasing fruit in your life, as described in Galatians 5:22–23. If you're not sure how mature you are or your partner is, ask your pastor or some older Christian whose judgment you trust.

14. *Can you accept and appreciate each other's family?* We are part of our families, and our families are part of us— whether we like them or not. You don't have to like them, but you do have to accept them, because that's essentially the same as accepting your partner.

15. *Do you have unresolved relationships in your past?* Love on the rebound is notoriously unstable. You both ought to be able to talk freely about "those who went before." You don't need to talk in detail, but if you just can't talk (or can't stop talking), you may be emotionally stuck in an earlier era. The past needs to be put entirely into the past.

16. *Is sex under control?* If not, it's an unhealthy sign for your future. You'll have to control yourselves many times, in many ways—including sexually—when you're married. If you can't do it now, you may be unable to do it later. This is not to suggest that you won't have a battle to control sex. The question is, who is winning the battle?

17. *Have you spent enough time together?* I don't consider any factor more critical than time. You can't really know each other deeply if you haven't had enough of it. How much is enough? As a rule of thumb, I'd say a year of real closeness is the minimum. In this amount of time you can get beyond the first blinding effects of love and see more clearly what you are committing yourself to.

18. *Have you fought and forgiven?* Walter Trobisch, who has written wisely on marriage, said that a couple should summer together and winter together. Anybody can get along when the sun is shining. Learning to accept and forgive when you have been hurt requires much more of the stuff that makes happy marriages. In a week of crisis you learn more about each other than in a month of happiness. If you cannot forgive, if you hold grudges, if you use "the silent treatment" to get your way, or if disagreement makes you lose your sanity—then you are not ready for marriage. Conflicts will come. You must have a way to overcome them.

19. *Have you talked about each area of your future life?* When you're far along in your relationship, and quite serious, you need to systematically discuss your future life. Finances, lifestyle, sexual expectations, jobs, children, parents—these and all other areas ought to be talked over in some detail. You'll be talking about these things if and when you're married, and you had better find out whether you can communicate. A helpful workbook is *Handbook for Engaged Couples.* Written by Bob and Alice Fryling and published by InterVarsity Press, this book gives you a list of issues to talk over.

20. *Have you had counseling?* Most couples would rather keep their relationship just to themselves. This kind of privacy, though comfortable, doesn't ultimately help. A trained outsider can see you from an angle you yourself can't see. A counselor can't tell you whether marriage is the right move. But he or she can help you explore questions you've ignored or problems you can't solve. Most pastors either do marriage counseling themselves or can recommend someone to go to. It's well worth paying for if there's a charge. If the

counseling is to be thorough, usually more than one session is necessary.

These twenty questions don't make a test you can grade. Each question is important enough that a marriage could fail on it. Each one must be considered with great care by both of you as you approach a final decision.

On the other hand, you don't have to be perfect or have a perfect relationship to make a happy and fruitful marriage. If marriage required perfection, all of us would fail.

What do you do if, approaching your wedding day, you aren't sure you're doing the right thing? You should, I believe, treat your doubts as an opportunity to prayerfully think of your partner, perhaps with the help of the previous twenty questions. Ask yourself whether you want to make this person "the right one" for life. Ask yourself whether you can stick to a lifetime with this person—and whether you want to stick to a lifetime with this person "in sickness and health, for better or worse, rich or poor."

Nobody should say "I do" just because he or she thinks it's too late to back out. Waiting a little longer is always better than going ahead with a ceremony you have serious doubts about. As embarrassing and troublesome as it is, a delay in your plans is not the end of the world. Of course, you have to make a choice at some point, and you will never eliminate all uncertainty. But sometimes extra time can help you be clearer about your choice.

Marriage is too good to enter into in the wrong way. The right way is with joy, love, and confidence that you are ready for whatever the future holds with "the right one."

The good news for Christians is that they do not have to make this choice alone. God's Spirit helps those who look to him for help, giving them wisdom and discernment in making decisions. God usually doesn't give the right answer; he does infallibly stand beside us to help us.

And there is more good news. Our uncertainty does not last indefinitely, as it does for those who do not know God. We do not have to spend our entire lives wondering if we made the right choice—if "the right one" might not be, in fact, some other woman or man. We suffer through uncertainty, but only for a time. Our wedding day brings joy partly because we believe we are ending the period of uncertainty and entering a period of absolute certainty. We have found "the right one." God himself stamps his approval on our marriage.

10. Pregnancy

I'm so afraid I'm pregnant! What should I do?

Q: In high school, I was the "nice girl." I kept this reputation, and loved it. After graduation I was college-bound—to a Christian college. Boy, were my parents proud! My older sisters had given them problems all through high school, but not me—I was their obedient angel.

So I was a freshman in college, miles and miles from home. I was having a blast with my new freedom. Along the road of my new life, I met a guy, a real nice, attractive, and mysterious guy. After a few months it became apparent that we were attracted to each other. One night he almost took my virginity, but I pushed him away. I was scared to death. He left me pretty upset that night, but I didn't want to end our relationship.

Another night he called and said he was coming over to pick me up. He wanted me to stay overnight. I thought, "How exciting, to wake up in someone's arms. A dream come true!" I had thought for quite awhile about giving up my virginity and had decided that I would probably do it sooner or later, so why not now?

You guessed it, I went to his house. I didn't have any birth control, so I told him that he'd better make sure I didn't get pregnant. He said not to worry, he would take care of it. So, that was one night. I had fun, but who says sin isn't fun? Another night he came over and we did it once again. By then

I was getting more and more nervous because my period was late.

To sum up my problem: I may be pregnant; my hometown would reject my baby; my parents may kick me out; I've lost my testimony. What do I do? I won't get an abortion. Where do I go to have the baby? I'm not sure I could handle adoption. I feel like I'm in a tornado, being spun around and around. I've heard of adoption agencies that are Christian and take babies such as mine. Where are they? Let me tell you, I am scared to death. I don't feel as if this is real—it's as if I'm trying to find a solution for a friend. Please help me decide what to do. I'm only eighteen!

A: The first thing you must do is see a doctor. Doctors not only know what to do medically, but they can usually direct women in your predicament to other kinds of help.

If you don't get the help you need from a doctor, try a pastor. Most of them, in my experience, aren't eagerly waiting to preach you a sermon. They want to help, and they can often refer you to the help you need.

If that doesn't work, try the yellow pages. Look under Abortion Alternatives, Adoption Services, or Birth Control Clinics. If you ask specifically for Christian help, they should try to find it for you.

Yes, there are Christian adoption agencies. Your doctor, pastor, or county health department ought to be able to put you in touch with one. (There's even a toll-free hotline you can call. An organization called Bethany Christian Services will give you free, confidential information and counsel and refer you to Christian help in your area. Their number is 1-800-BETHANY.)

You say you are not sure you can handle adoption; I'm glad you're aware of how difficult a choice that is. It hurts to give up one's own flesh and blood. It hurts deeply. Because of that, many girls in your situation choose to keep their babies. That can work, especially if you have loving parents who are willing to essentially raise your baby for you. But even so, becoming a single mother at eighteen will place severe demands on you.

A baby is not a doll, but a very demanding human being who causes considerable stress even for two mature parents. I believe that adoption, painful as it is, is usually the best choice for a mother and baby in your situation. If you quit school to take care of your child, you might end up in perpetual poverty, unless you have some other source of substantial income. Even then, you'd be forcing yourself to grow up very suddenly into motherhood.

Not many of your friends would be able to relate to your responsibilities as a mother. Not many guys your age would want to date you. In many cases these facts are very difficult for a single, young mother to accept, and she passes her unhappiness on to the baby. I am not underestimating the difficulty of saying good-bye, forever, to your own beautiful child. Unfortunately, your situation does not offer a painless option.

It would be hard to give up your baby after carrying it for nine months, but you can do it with a greater sense of confidence if you know that your child will grow up in a loving, mature Christian family. Babies are so in demand now that you can probably choose the kind of parents you want for your child. If you don't like the adoption agencies you contact, consider private adoption. Your doctor or lawyer may have a file of letters from young couples who wish they could adopt a baby: You could actually choose who would raise and love your child.

It doesn't sound as though you have any interest in marrying the baby's father—nor should you, based on the shallow relationship you've formed. However, babies cost money, a lot of money, and he is legally responsible. I suppose it's inevitable that girls get stuck with most of the pain when they get pregnant outside marriage. But the guy should at least assume some of the bills, especially if you choose to raise the child yourself. The "experts" can counsel you about how to involve him.

You'll need a place to go. There are Christian homes

where you can have your baby. The Salvation Army runs several, for instance. But your first choice should be your family. Sooner or later you have to face them. It might as well be sooner. Usually, though not always, the family will get over their shock and disappointment and will welcome their daughter (and sister) back with loving arms. That's how families are meant to be, and most live up to it.

God will welcome you with loving arms, too. He's not even shocked by your behavior. He knows precisely the value of a "good girl" reputation. He loves you. He is not callous. He feels your pain. He wants to forgive you and to help you live through this experience. He wants to help you start building your life again.

You can't ever go back to your high school days, but maybe that's just as well. It sounds as though your "good girl" reputation was just an outfit to try on for size, to take off when you got bored with it. You were playing a game. But life is no game, as you are learning the hard way. You don't pick up the pieces and put them away after you lose. You live with the consequences of your choices all through life.

You will never forget this experience. Its memory will be with you when you reach eighty. That doesn't mean, however, that your life is ruined. On the contrary, this could be the beginning of a much deeper and sounder way of life than you have experienced so far. Many people are able to look back on hard times such as yours and say, "My life really began then."

Will you keep trying on outfits? Or will you turn to God and ask him to lead you through this, forming you into a person with a deep and permanent commitment to him?

Why is abortion so bad?

Q: When I was fifteen, I got pregnant. The guy who got me pregnant said I would have to have an abortion. He gave me no other choices.

The day of the abortion, I was a little scared, not knowing what to expect. The people at the clinic were exceptionally nice to me. The whole thing only took about fifteen minutes, and it wasn't very painful.

Now, two years later, I am wondering why everyone thinks it's so wrong. I have no regrets or guilty feelings. Everything worked out perfectly. I didn't even tell my parents. People are always saying that abortion is wrong. I was the mother, and I think it was my choice. I think I made the best one. So why does everyone think that's so bad?

A: It all boils down to one question: Was that a baby inside you? If it was, then "everything worked out perfectly" isn't quite correct. Somebody—a very helpless somebody— died. It wasn't perfect for him or her. And since you were involved, it wasn't perfect for you—if that was a baby inside you.

If you think about it, the fact that you haven't felt guilty doesn't prove much. If you browse through your local newspaper you will read of people who have been convicted of terrible crimes but feel no regrets. Of course, feeling *guilty* wouldn't prove much either. The question isn't how you felt. The question is, What was that inside you?

I have deep respect for human life. As a Christian, I believe God has imprinted all human beings with his own image. We dare not kill human beings for our convenience. (See Genesis 9:6.) I believe that a fetus is a developing human being. From the moment of conception, a baby begins to develop very gradually; this development continues up to the point of birth and continues after birth. Everyone agrees that to kill a toddler is as wrong as to kill an adult—the fact that the child is less developed makes no difference. I think the same logic applies to unborn children.

The situation you found yourself in, pregnant and alone, must have been truly awful. The choice you made is understandable even if wrong. But understanding the agony you and others face shouldn't make us obscure the facts. So far I have not heard a convincing argument for why a baby yet unborn is not a baby. That's why, in a nutshell, "everyone thinks it's so bad."

What is it like to give up a baby for adoption?

Q: Just a few minutes ago I was lying on the couch reading a letter in your column from an eighteen-year-old girl who wrote about her boyfriend Ted and the fact that she is pregnant with someone else's baby. I felt there was something I wanted to share with her and anyone else in that situation.

About one year ago I was in the same position. Just like her, I was afraid to tell anybody. Finally, when I was seven months pregnant I went through the yellow pages of our local phone book and found an ad for Bethany Christian Services. I called the number, explained my situation, and was soon in touch with a counselor in Modesto, California. Linda explained to me that Bethany was designed to help unwed mothers through their pregnancy, in parenting, and in arranging adoptions. After talking to Linda I decided to move to Modesto and live in their maternity home. "The Master's House" is a very special place where I lived with nine other girls in similar situations to mine.

I chose to place my baby up for adoption. Linda continued to counsel with me through the entire pregnancy. Before my baby was born I read several letters from Christian couples looking to adopt a child. I chose one couple who I knew would give my baby everything I could not.

Finally the day came. I gave birth to an eight-pound baby boy. I named him Julian and we spent three days together in Modesto City Hospital. During those three days I really became attached to Julian. When the time came to say good-bye, it was the hardest thing I've ever had to do. I

LOVE, SEX & THE WHOLE PERSON

prayed that God would be with both of us and his adoptive parents for all the days of our lives.

The next few days after leaving the hospital were filled with much pain and many tears, but I wasn't alone. My houseparents, Linda, and a counselor in the Master's House all took the time to listen to me and comfort me during such a painful experience.

Finally, two days after I said good-bye to Julian in the hospital, I decided to sign the relinquishment papers. That very same night his adoptive parents picked him up from his foster home, and at 1:00 that morning I got a phone call from them. Oh, boy, they sure were excited about their new baby. They both assured me that they would do their best in raising him in a loving Christian home.

I wrote Julian a letter to explain my story to him and why I chose adoption. His parents and I continue to write back and forth. They send me pictures of him so I may see how much he is growing.

Julian turned sixteen weeks old on Christmas day. Although I was not able to spend Christmas with him, and many years will pass before I see my son again, he is the best gift I have ever received.

A: Thank you for your very moving letter. I got choked up reading it, and I'd bet many others will too. You've helped us all understand what it's like to go through an adoption.

I have another view of what you've done. Several years ago a couple in our Bible study group decided to pursue adoption after many painful years in which they were unable to conceive a child. We talked with them week by week as they searched for any possibility of a child. Sometimes they—and we—almost despaired of their finding a baby. Finally, a young woman like you contacted them.

Through months of pregnancy we prayed for her and her child. One evening the news came that she was in labor. Our friends dropped everything and flew to the hospital, which was in another state. Would it really happen? After all the prayers, all the hoping and waiting, would our friends have a child of their own? We agonized with them, knowing quite well how difficult it would be for the mother to give up her child. (Having children of our own, we can imagine—barely.) A few days later we welcomed them home. They had in their arms a beautiful little girl named Natalie. We all went to the courtroom to celebrate on the day of her official adoption.

Since then we've watched Natalie grow up. We greet her in church most Sundays. We've seen her gain a little sister (through the same means). We see how happy she and her sister are, how well cared for they have been, and we see most of all the happiness in the faces of their parents. It's hard for me to perceive anything but good in this. I know that from the mother's point of view it must have been very, very difficult. I certainly can sympathize with those who decide to keep their children. But having seen my friends' experience, I'm definitely biased in favor of adoption. It's an unimaginably wonderful gift to people who long to have children. Most often, I believe, it's also a gift to the child.

11. Sexually Transmitted Diseases

Can a Christian cope with herpes?

Q: I have had herpes for three years. I am twenty-six. I am a Christian. Where sex and men are concerned, I have been among the worst of sinners. The struggle to forgive myself and to receive God's forgiveness has been a real battle. I want to tell others how I am beginning to feel free, to have peace.

Having herpes means being branded. With each outbreak the ugliness and shame of your sin slaps you in the face. You feel unworthy of real love—the glowing prospect of a solid marriage dims and withers before you. How could any man love one so marked with the recurring reminder of sin? For a long time I felt like damaged freight.

This is twisted truth. The moment I put my heart in God's and trusted him above and beyond my own ability to "be good," that brand, that herpes, became no longer a mark of sin but a mark of God's fathering hand. For me now, every outbreak is a fresh message from God, reminding me that he loved me enough to discipline me before I could discipline myself. He also uses the outbreaks as a signal to me that I am not taking care of myself, or that there is something between us that needs taking care of. I have lived in more continuous communion with him since contracting herpes than I might have if I did not have outbreaks. And I know without doubt that God will heal me completely when the herpes is no longer of such good use to him for my sake.

Herpes has restricted my marriage prospects. Many Christian men would be appalled at me. I'll tell you something. I have much less chance of choosing the wrong mate because of it. Way to go, God!

A: Thanks for the message. Your words say a great deal more than I could to those who share your problem. They also say a lot to those who have never given herpes a thought. Sex is not "playing around." Possibly nothing we do has so many profound implications for our futures—both good and evil. God can use all things for his good, as he evidently is doing with you. But there are easier ways to learn these lessons.

I've emphasized that sex is a deep, spiritual sharing between two people. The bond has profound personal implications, whether we want it to or not. Your letter reminds me that sex is also a deep *physical* sharing between two people. Whatever sexual disease one has, the other may contract. This bond, too, has profound personal implications.

A Christian with AIDS?

Q: Two weeks ago I went with my Campus Crusade group to hear Josh McDowell. He spoke about many things but cleverly saved the best for last. To over six hundred students, counselors, and parents in a huge Baptist church, Josh talked about "Why Wait?" Everyone listened as Josh rattled off terrifying statistics about sexually transmitted diseases. You could hear a pin drop; it was completely silent. I wondered how many people, like me, listened because of purely personal reasons. How many of them were fearful for things they'd already done? Damage they can't undo to their young bodies?

LOVE, SEX & THE WHOLE PERSON

I am only eighteen years old. It is not that I live in New York or Chicago where AIDS runs rampant; in fact, the place where I live may not even be on the map! It is the fact that I have had eight sexual partners in the past year, from all backgrounds. I thought nothing of it at the time; I was just "sowing wild oats," blowing off steam, looking for something I wasn't supposed to have. I had never done those things (drinking, sex) before, and I don't now. There was just approximately a year in my life when I took leave of my senses and went literally wild.

Now I'll be wondering about that year for perhaps fifteen more (Josh said that AIDS can stay dormant for that long). It wasn't Josh's "nightmare" lecture that got me to stop indulging in sex. But it was Josh who scared me to death. Before, I never thought about it. Young people, especially Christians, think they're immune to serious diseases and anything fatal. If you don't go to a Christian college, it's easy to give in to the "college mentality"—eat, drink, and sleep with Mary. At least for a while you want to try what you never have done before. After all, everyone else does. You figure, "I'm young—young people are supposed to do this, aren't they?"

It's not a matter of feeling guilty. I've worked that out with God, and I know I'm forgiven. I was young and (at the risk of using a cliché) naïve. I really was! I'd never even heard of this killer until two years ago, much less understood it.

I don't think I'm overreacting. Nowadays, you can't overreact. Any time you sleep with someone, even if you know him, you're at risk. Knowing I was forgiven, I looked forward to a future doing what God wanted me to do. To have a husband, a best friend, with whom I could make passionate love whenever we wanted for the rest of our lives. Now, when I think about the future, I get scared. I get depressed. I don't see anything.

If I'm in this situation, others must be too. This is never discussed: What does a Christian do with AIDS? I have Christian friends who have been "good boys and girls." Why couldn't I? Can you imagine how scared I am? I need, I suppose, something positive. I feel like my future may not be.

A: First let's talk medicine. It's true, as Josh McDowell said, that AIDS can lie dormant in your body for a long time. However, that doesn't mean you have to wait fifteen years to find out whether you have problems. You can be tested accurately within a few months of your last possible exposure. The test will tell you whether or not you have been infected with the AIDS virus. I'd strongly recommend you get the test. You'd be far better off facing one excruciating moment of truth than a hundred such crises for years to come.

If you have been infected, you need time to face the very real possibility of death. If you haven't—and going by the percentages, you probably haven't—then you can truly put your past behind you. So long as you're unsure, every cold will be a crisis—is it the beginning of AIDS? Your uncertainty will block any serious relationships with the opposite sex. How can you think about marriage if you don't know whether marriage might bring the death of your husband, since you might infect him? Uncertainty is much worse than certainty, no matter how bad the certainty turns out to be.

I agree with you that overreacting to AIDS is impossible for someone considering whether to be sexually promiscuous. As Katie Leishman put it in the *Atlantic*, if there were a thousand guns on a table and only one of them was loaded, how many people would pick up one, point it at their head, and pull the trigger, if the prize were a toaster? No matter how small the risk of infection may be, AIDS's life-and-death consequences make cheap thrills extremely expensive.

However, for people like you, looking at their past, it is possible to overreact to AIDS. There is a real possibility you've been infected with a disease that will kill you. But there's a much better chance that you haven't. I think you've let the situation get out of perspective, so much so that your fears have taken over your common sense. Common sense says, get tested. Then decide what to do next.

Now let's talk spiritually. The apostle Paul wrote, in Romans 8:38, "I am convinced that neither death nor life, neither angels nor demons, neither the present nor the future, nor any powers, neither height nor depth, nor anything else in all creation, will be able to separate us from the love of God that is in Christ Jesus our Lord."

Neither death nor life can keep you from experiencing God's love. If you have contracted AIDS, you will experience God's love in death soon. If you don't get AIDS, you will experience God's love in death sooner or later, for we all die. Either way, Paul's words put AIDS in perspective. Paul is saying that the great variable in life isn't a deadly disease. The great variable is whether you have accepted God's forgiveness and salvation. He is saying that there is something far more powerful than AIDS: God's love.

That means you do have a future, one that doesn't depend on what your test results show. You have a future with God, in his love. You ask what a Christian with AIDS should do? First he needs to confess and repent for any wrong actions he's done. He needs to ask for, and receive, God's forgiveness. If he's done that, he can do just what a Christian with cancer, or Alzheimer's, or any deadly disease would do. He can draw closer to God, through prayer and worship and Bible reading, in order to experience more deeply God's love in life and in death.

I don't know, of course, what your future will look like. I hope you don't have AIDS and can go on to experience the future you've dreamed of—a joyful life of living and loving with one chosen person. Whether or not that comes, however, I know God has a future for you. His dreams for your life are better than your wildest dreams. None of us can see what he has in store for us. We have to live by faith, until those dreams—*his* dreams—become reality.

12. Relating to Parents

How do you handle parents who are determined to keep you away from someone you love?

Q: I'm a senior in high school, and I'm in love with a freshman girl from another school. Her name is Stacy. We started dating about ten months ago. We went out about once a week, and I went to church with her on Sunday nights. If some type of special occasion came up, we usually went to that, too. We really had fun together. I had dated other girls before, but this was entirely different. Our relationship wasn't built around sex or anything like that. We enjoyed just being together, talking and doing things.

At first her mother and stepfather were very nice. I liked them a lot. But after a few months they seemed to change their attitude. They felt we had been talking on the phone too much, so they said we could only talk every other night. Well, I could understand how they felt and I even agreed with them. Not long afterward they said that we were seeing each other too often, so they cut that down to once a week, and I could only go to church with her about once a month.

Stacy and I wondered why her parents were doing this. We are both Christians, and we know that God is our shepherd and that he watches over us. But everything seemed to take a turn for the worse.

About five months ago I attended Sunday evening services at the church Stacy attends, because a friend invited me. The following Monday Stacy called me. She was crying, very upset. Her parents had said that by coming to church without calling or asking them, I was sneaking around their backs. They said we couldn't date, call, write, or see each other in any way. Nothing!

Two weeks later Stacy called me and said that her parents wanted to talk to me. I went and talked, but nothing changed. They still felt the same way.

One week Stacy was very sick, so I sent her some flowers. I thought nothing of it at the time. The next day Stacy's mother called me at work. She said that if I called, wrote, or tried to get in touch with Stacy again, they would punish her for it. That really hurt me; I didn't know what to do or who to turn to.

It's been almost five months now since we've had a date or spent any time together. We still feel the same toward each other, and we want to have a relationship, but her parents won't allow that. We can't understand what—if anything— we did wrong, or why her parents feel the way they do. We can't understand why they can't forgive us or understand how we feel. Since they've stopped us from dating, Stacy hasn't been able to get along with either of them. They both insist they have nothing against me, but neither of them will even speak to me.

What should we do? How can we get through to Stacy's parents?

A: Right now you can't do much. There are two sides to every story, and I imagine that if I talked to Stacy's parents they might tell a different version of what has happened. I notice, for example, that you and Stacy seem to have communicated together despite her parents' wish that you not do so.

Still, I have no trouble believing that her parents have overreacted. Many parents are scared to death these days. They read the newspapers and talk to other parents, and they fear their children will get into trouble. Stacy's parents may just be scared human beings who don't have a well-thought-out policy. They care about Stacy deeply, and it probably frightens them to see her so involved with a guy.

How do you handle people who are terrified? You don't argue with them, because if they're scared, they can't think straight. You try to calm them down first. Later you reason with them.

That probably means you and Stacy should hang it up for now. Give her parents a good long chance to relax, then ask to see them again. Perhaps in a few months they'll be ready to talk.

It would help if Stacy could get along with her parents. Fighting is bound to reinforce their fears that she's out of control. If she's peaceful, cheerful, and obedient, they'll be less likely to worry.

If some adult could be a mediator, that might help too. He or she would have to be someone Stacy's parents trust, as well as someone who knows you and Stacy well. If you're the person Stacy's parents are scared of, they might find it hard to listen calmly to you. A go-between might help them relax and hear the message. A go-between might also help you understand whatever message Stacy's parents are trying to send to you.

I think there's a very good chance that, with patience, you will win Stacy's parents over. But there's no guarantee. They may remain irrational until their dying day. If so, Stacy will have to live with that. And you, if you really love her, will have to live with it too.

The Bible calls on children to honor and obey their parents. It also calls on parents to be reasonable. Each person is meant to keep his or her side of the bargain, no matter how the other person acts. As long as Stacy lives under her parents' roof, she ought to honor and obey them, no matter how unreasonable they are, so long as they don't tell her to do something that's wrong.

That seems pretty unfair, but there's logic behind it. It's not that parents always know best. Sometimes they don't. But parent-child relationships are a building block of society, and, even more, they are a building block of a person's psychology. Disrupted relationships with parents last a lifetime. You never really get over them.

Believe me, you don't want to marry someone with a messed-up family background if you can help it. You'll end up reliving those problems again and again. You can look on this situation as a test. Solve this problem, and you and Stacy can solve any problem together.

You say you know that the Lord is your shepherd, and that he watches over you. Practically speaking, that means that if your relationship with Stacy is really of lifelong importance, you won't miss out on it. God will open a way for you to get together. It might be next week, it might be next year, it might be even further into the future. You can afford to wait, if necessary, for God is in control.

He knows what or who is good for you, far better than you do. It might be Stacy. It might be someone else. As long as your life belongs to him, you won't miss out on the best.

That's what can give you and Stacy the courage to honor and obey her parents. You don't have to believe that her parents are right. You just have to believe that God is in control. He puts a priority on positive, peaceful relationships within your family. If you live by his priorities, you'll see him work things out for you. When you're dealing with a painful and irrational situation, it takes faith to believe that. But that's what living by faith is all about: trusting God even when you don't see how things will work out.

My dad's curfew rule seems unfair!

Q: My dad makes me get home from a date by midnight, which I think is ridiculous. A lot of times I have to leave a party when it's hardly beginning. He says he doesn't want me to get into trouble, but I'm old enough to know what I want to do. If I decide I'm going to do something, I can do it before 12:00 as well as after 12:00. The clock doesn't influence that. I know I'm supposed to obey until I'm on my own, but do rules like this make any sense?

A: They wouldn't if everything you did were based on calm, rational decisions, regardless of the circumstances. But I doubt everything is.

One guy told me this story: "I was 150 miles from home, and completely alone on the beach with this girl. No one in that area knew me. All the instincts for sex were there. At the time it seemed like making love would be perfect, wonderful. There was nothing stopping us. The only thing that held me back was the Christian teaching I'd had in church, from Campus Life, etc. That teaching didn't make much sense to me then, but it left a nagging doubt in my mind that wouldn't let me go beyond certain limits. It wasn't a rational thing, but now I'm very glad it was there."

That's one example of how decisions get influenced by factors that don't fit a neat, logical equation. Sex drives aren't logical, and sometimes an "irrational" factor like a parental rule can help you deal with an "irrational" sexy situation. I've had people tell me later that parental rules they hated at the time saved them a lot of grief.

Obviously, if you let yourself go for long periods of time in a dark, intimate atmosphere with a member of the opposite sex, a decision you made earlier about how far to go might get lost in the excitement. And a lot of those "intimate moments" come past midnight.

That's probably what your father has in mind. I'd imagine he remembers some postmidnight experiences of his own and would just as soon have you avoid them.

What he may not understand is that times have changed, and there's more to do after midnight than make out. I'd recommend you sit down with him and explain exactly what you'd like to do after midnight, why you don't like leaving parties by 12:00, etc. (Incidentally, if you haven't proved that you know how to get in at 12:00 when that's the set limit, don't expect him to trust you with more time.) If he still won't bend—well, you'll live. It's just possible your dad knows you better than you know yourself and has made a rule that will help you.

In a few more years you'll make your own decisions about when to get in. In the meantime, it's not a bad idea to get used to following unpleasant rules. You'll probably be doing that at your job for several more years, too—like forty or fifty more.

What if *parents* have immoral sexual habits?

Q: I am a fifteen-year-old girl who has a problem not many of my friends understand. My mom and her boyfriend started dating about three years ago. We soon started spending the night at his house. This didn't bother me because my mom and I slept in the front bedroom. But then they started sleeping together. This also didn't bother me much, until one night I went back there to ask my mother something and her boyfriend came out of the bathroom with his underwear on (and just his underwear). Then I soon caught them having sex.

I know that they don't plan on getting married because we have often talked about it. My question is, what should I do about this situation so that my mom will know how I feel without starting a huge argument? My mom and I have an open relationship, but I just don't think I could come out and tell her.

This same thing happens between my dad and his girlfriend. But my dad and I don't talk much.

A: You're not the first person to become like a "parent" to her parents. In some ways it's inevitable: parents are not perfect, and as you grow up you're bound to find some areas where you know things they ought to know. This generation is probably the first one in American memory in which some kids have better morals about sex and drugs than some of their parents. But other generations of kids faced parents who were racists, or alcoholics, or gossips.

Your mom and dad are not very likely to listen to your convictions objectively. It's hard to reverse the roles. Fair or not, when they see you, they see the baby they diapered. So it's hard for them to believe you could know more than they do. Still, it does happen that kids convince their parents. If you can't talk to your mom about it, why don't you write her a letter? Or clip out an article on the subject and give it to her? She may be more willing to talk than you realize. If she is, she'll respond to your note.

Perhaps the most effective argument you can make is the practice of your Christian faith. The truth is, God is more likely to convince your mom than you are. Pray for her. Let her see and hear the way God works in you.

Another powerful argument is that of your feelings. If your mom is a typical parent, she really cares for you. You should let her know how confusing and upsetting her sex life is for you. Tell her how it makes you *feel* and what it's doing to her relationship with you. That may not change her mind about right and wrong, but it could help her change her lifestyle.

Finally, realize that you may not change your mom. Most kids can't change their parents. You have about three more years to live at home, and although that's a long time, it's not a lifetime. Work on surviving. Go out of your way to develop some adult friends at church or in the neighborhood who model a good marriage and family life for you. Develop friends whom you trust, whom you can talk to honestly. If life gets too confusing, don't hesitate to see a counselor for help.

Make up your mind that you will love your mom but not imitate her in every aspect of life. When you see behavior you don't want to follow, mark it in your mind: "When I'm in that spot, I will try to do it differently."

13. Sex in Our Heads: Lust, Pornography, Dreams

What does the Bible mean by "lust"?

Q: I am a nineteen-year-old virgin. It has not been easy to stay this way, but I am a very disciplined person, and I have managed to control my actions. I felt pretty good about myself until I read Matthew 5:28, in which Jesus tells us that anyone who lusts after a woman with his eye has already committed adultery in his heart. I have found it totally impossible to keep from thinking about sex, especially when I am around females. This passage also tells us that masturbation is obviously wrong, because when a person masturbates, he or she is thinking lustfully and is usually fantasizing about someone in particular.

This means that from the time I reach puberty (twelve–fourteen) until the time I get married (probably about twenty-five, at the earliest) I am not only supposed to keep from having or thinking about sex, but I can't even masturbate, not even once. Why would God create all this sexual energy in me and never allow me to release it? I find this to be totally unnatural, illogical, impossible, and ungodly. I feel extremely guilty. I am severely depressed and I don't know if I even believe in God at all. I have even started avoiding girls to keep from thinking about sex. Please help!

A: I believe you've misunderstood what Jesus said, though it's a misinterpretation lots of people make. If you look at the context Jesus spoke in, you see that he took up a whole list of topics—murder, adultery, revenge, generosity, prayer, fasting—and went through it attacking the attitudes of religious people who thought they had it all together. Jesus told them that their goodness wasn't good enough. People who were proud of themselves because, for example, they'd never committed adultery, should see that their thoughts and desires needed to be as pure as their actions.

"Be perfect," Jesus went on to say, "as your heavenly Father is perfect" (Matthew 5:48). If we had been able to live up to that, Jesus wouldn't have had to die on the cross for our sins. But he did. None of us can live up to all God expects. Jesus wanted people to understand how much they need God.

Some of us may not need forgiveness for our sexual behavior, but all of us need forgiveness for our sexual desires. I have wrong desires, you have wrong desires, your pastor has wrong desires. They're not wrong just because Jesus said they were wrong; they're wrong because they're evil and destructive. Rather than feeling satisfied with ourselves, we're to come closer to God in recognition of our constant need for forgiveness and healing. That's the first point I want to make. Don't get angry with God because he expects the world of you. Come closer to him. Learn that you can't live without him. Learn that he wants to give you the world.

There's a second way in which you've misunderstood Jesus: I believe you've misunderstood the command not to lust. "Lust," in English, usually suggests mental pictures about sex. In Greek, though, the word (*epithymia*) doesn't have that connotation. It just means "powerful desire." It's not even a negative word. It can be a beautiful desire, as it was when Jesus told his disciples at the Last Supper, "I have eagerly desired [lusted] to eat this Passover with you . . ." (Luke 22:15).

So you have to look at the context to understand what "lust" really means. That's not crystal clear in Matthew, but it seems to be "committing adultery in your heart." Your heart, according to the Bible, isn't composed of thoughts that flit through your mind. Your heart is your core identity; it's the direction you choose to point your life. I think Jesus is referring to times when one would commit adultery if he could.

Suppose you go out with a girl. You get sexually excited to the point where you're ready and willing to go all the way. But something stops you. Perhaps it's fear. Perhaps it's *her* willpower: she said no. Perhaps you just got interrupted when her parents came home. For whatever reason, you didn't go all the way. How do you think about yourself afterwards? Some would think, "Whew, I'm still pure. I have never failed." If they heard about other people who were sexually involved, they'd feel superior.

Jesus is taking on such a response. He is saying, "Oh, no. You're no better than they are. You wanted to do it. Your heart is just as rotten as theirs. You need God's healing and forgiveness just as much as they do."

This kind of lust could happen even with someone you don't know—a girl you watch every day in class, thinking about what you'd like to do with her. Are you better than the person who actually does it? No, you'd like to do it, so you need forgiveness and help too. Your actions aren't wrong, but your desires are.

That's what Jesus is getting at, I believe. I don't think he's trying to get you to stop being a sexual creature. I don't think he's suggesting that when you look at a beautiful girl you should avoid sexual attraction. I don't think he's talking about masturbation. I think he's talking about your heart— that is, the fundamental desires you choose to center your life on.

When sexual thoughts come into your mind, it's quite possible to thank God for beautiful girls and for sexuality and just to feel good about being alive as a male in a world full of sexual beauty. You can imagine how wonderful it will be to be married someday. That's good and healthy, I believe. There's nothing evil about those desires.

What's not good is to take those thoughts and build on

them, manipulate them, obsess yourself with the thought of how much joy you'd get from going to bed with one of those girls. Whether you act on your desires or not, you've made sex into something dirty. Jesus doesn't want you to turn off your sexuality (as though you could). He wants you to turn it in the proper direction. And, always, he wants you to turn toward him. Let me say again: all of us are sick and in need of his healing and forgiveness.

Why didn't God make it easy? Why not give us sexual desires on our wedding day, and not before? Why not take away our attraction to people other than our spouses? Why not, for that matter, take away our tendency for greed, so that we wouldn't think somebody else's Porsche was particularly attractive? I don't know why. You can play the "Why didn't God do it differently?" game for a long time and not come up with any answers. I do know I wouldn't like to be without sexual desires. I like being a human being, hard as it is. I'm thankful God trusted me with the challenge. I'm equally thankful that God picks me up when I fail to live my life the way I should.

Is it sinful to think about sex?

Q: Is it sinful to think about sex? I know that sex is a very special, intimate way for a husband and wife to express their love for each other. That's how it's going to be in my life. But I am curious about sex. I wonder how it feels physically and emotionally. I wonder what it would be like to have it with any of the guys that are very special to me. When I find myself being curious, I think I'm being lustful and sinful. So I ask God's forgiveness and push the thoughts back. Sometimes I encourage these thoughts and go into my own little fantasy. Then I really have to repent. But most of the time it's just curiosity. Am I lusting? If not, what do I do when I feel guilty about my curiosity?

A: It's very natural and even healthy to be curious about sex and to think about it. I doubt that anyone ever woke up on his wedding day and said, "Hey, sex! Somebody said you have sex when you're married! I wonder what it's all about." If someone had thought that little about it, I would worry.

It's very difficult, though, to say exactly when a thought stops being innocent. Some thoughts are obviously good, and others definitely bad. A million thoughts pass through my mind every day, and I have a hard time telling you just exactly where they turn from "just curiosity" to "sin."

The Bible tells us not to lust (Matthew 5:28) but doesn't define exactly what lust is. It tells us to concentrate on thoughts that are uplifting (Philippians 4:8) but not whether it's sinful to let a few "neutral" thoughts slip through the cracks.

I think there's a reason for this imprecision. I don't think God wants us to spend a lot of time studying our own thoughts. My belief is that you should work at keeping your mind on things that uplift you but not worry too much about thought control. For one thing, you can't totally succeed at it: Did you ever try not to think of pink elephants? And for another thing, God seems to have made your mind so it is "on" all the time; I think that's related to a gift called imagination, and I'm sure those stray thoughts often lead to creativity.

But there are some thoughts that do harm us. We ought to watch for those and kick them out of our minds. Let me suggest some general guidelines.

1. *Thoughts are bad when they hurt your relationship with another person.* If wondering about sex with guys you know carries over into the daytime or becomes the main way you think of them, then it is time to stop. People are not sex objects. You can't have a really good relationship with anyone whom you constantly think of that way.

2. *Thoughts are bad when they distract you from real life.* If you are in a dream world, you can't cope with reality. If you're constantly thinking about sex, it will take away from

the time you spend thinking about things that will genuinely uplift you.

3. *Thoughts are bad when they increase your desire to do something you know is wrong.* This is a little tricky to apply in the area of sex, because what is wrong to desire outside of marriage is quite right to desire in marriage. Sex within marriage is wonderful, and I can't see anything wrong with thinking about it. But if thinking about it is making you more likely to give in to temptation before marriage, those thoughts ought to be kicked out.

In general, I can't see anything wrong with a thought that just pops into your head. It's what you do with the thought that is right or wrong. Martin Luther once said that we can't keep birds from flying over our heads but we can keep them from nesting in our hair. It is quite normal to have curious thoughts about sex come into your head—all kinds of thoughts, some quite bizarre. I don't think this means you are doing anything wrong.

Everybody has weeds come up in his mental garden. When you feel guilty about the kind of thinking you've been doing, check out the thoughts; there may be nothing wrong with them at all. Sex is an emotional subject and often brings strange feelings with it. If you believe that there is something wrong with your thoughts, simply say something like this to God: "Father, I'm really grateful you've given me a conscience and have helped me to recognize that these thoughts aren't doing me good but harm. I'm really sorry that I let my mind wander so far in this direction. Thank you for your forgiveness. Please help me to weed out these thoughts and create in me an interest in thinking about more worthwhile things."

Is it wrong to read magazines like *Playboy*?

Q: I'm a sophomore in high school. I'm trying to find out if reading magazines like *Playboy* or *Penthouse* is wrong. My friends look at them, and I keep telling them it's wrong. They tell me that looking at those pictures is just like looking at something from nature. I wish you could help me.

A: I'll believe your friends are just nature lovers when I see them avidly passing around pictures of a naked cow moose. The human body is a part of nature, but it's much more than nature.

Isn't it strange that you can buy pictures of nude women at any drugstore, yet if you asked a girl at school to take her clothes off for you in public, she'd consider it an insult, and probably think you were emotionally disturbed? By and large, people prefer to keep their clothes on. It gives them a sense of privacy.

I do believe there is a place for nudity in art that celebrates the beauty and sensuality of the human body. But I seriously doubt, despite all claims to the contrary, that people read the skin mags because they're interested in art. They read them to look at the pictures, and they look at the pictures to get themselves sexually excited.

God meant sex to be an intensely personal communication between a man and a woman who love each other and are committed to that love. *Playboy* and *Penthouse* simulate the experience through a "relationship" between a man and colored dots on a piece of paper. This kind of soft-core pornography is a poor substitute for real sex. Winning a woman's love takes time and character. But it takes only a few bucks to get a magazine. There is no commitment, no love, no communication, no mutuality.

I am not on a crusade against *Playboy* and its like. There

are worse things in the world. But I do think one is wise to stay away from them. Like any cheap substitute, *Playboy* tends to detract from the real thing. If you get used to snacking on Sugar Crisps, you'll be less likely to go to the effort to cook vegetables for supper. If you get used to thinking about sex in the quick, easy, uninvolved skin-mag way, you'll have a hard time mustering the energy to take it more seriously in relationships with real live men and women. Skin mags are the junk food of sex. They seem relatively harmless, but they are habit forming, at least for some. And habits are powerful.

Of course, you find the instant-gratification, no-commitment version of sex in places other than drugstore racks. Movies often throw in sex with no reason other than to prove they can do what television can't (yet). It's a rare popular book that doesn't have the same kinds of throw-away scenes. And for my money, television is the dirtiest medium of all. There's no explicit sex and very little nudity, but how they make up for it in the way they talk! Sex is portrayed exclusively (and frequently) as something to be laughed at, to manipulate someone with, or to have instant fun with.

So you won't be able to keep yourself pure from a quick-and-easy view of sex—it's all around you. The best you can do is minimize its influence.

You don't always know in advance what you're going to see when you go to a flick or turn on the TV. But you do know what you'll find when you open a *Playboy* or a *Penthouse*. It's not helping you, and it can hurt you. My advice is to stay away from such cheap thrills.

Are sexual dreams sinful?

Q: I've been having sex-driven dreams for a long time. Before I accepted Jesus I had them too, but they didn't usually bother me then. Now they do. I've asked God to cleanse me and take these dreams from me, but they don't seem to stop.

Is this a sin? Is there anything I can do? I honestly know that love is more than just sex, but should I ask for forgiveness every time I have these dreams?

A: The best thing you can do is relax. Love is, as you say, more than sex—but that doesn't mean there is something wrong with sex. Most people, especially when they're young, have a lot of sexual tension inside. It's a result of certain hormones that God gives us. The tension comes out in the awkward way we act around the opposite sex, in our fantasies, in our dreams. There is nothing wrong with the tension—in fact, it's good, as it shows God is entrusting you with a great new area of life to explore.

So don't worry about it. Many (if not most) people have such dreams, at least occasionally. And I don't see how God could hold you responsible for something you can't help.

The more you relax about your God-given sexual impulses, the less preoccupying they'll become.

14. Sexual Abuse

A note to victims of sexual abuse.

If you have been the victim of sexual abuse—rape, incest, or any sexual intimacy you felt forced into—you have the power to help yourself. Sexual abuse is a far more common occurrence than many people realize. Usually the experience results in fear, confusion, and guilt feelings. It can seriously affect your personality development and relationships with other people. The problems will usually not go away by themselves.

If this has happened to you, you have suffered enough. You need to get help from a professional counselor immediately. Start by talking to your pastor or your school counselor and asking for a referral. You don't even need to explain what the problem is. Just say that you need some professional counseling about a personal matter and would like a recommendation about a counselor.

Failing that, look in the telephone book. In the listings for your county or state government you should find a listing for mental-health services. In the yellow pages you can look under Marriage, Family, and Child Counselors, or under Mental Health Services. With the anonymity of a telephone call, you can ask (without telling your name if you don't want to) for a referral to a professional counselor for sexual abuse.

Making this call may be very difficult, but you need to do it. And in the long run, you will be very glad you did.

I was a rape victim. How can I deal with my feelings of guilt?

Q: I keep reading your magazine, I've looked in back issues, I've read Christian books, and I've talked to a few Christian counselors. Nobody seems to directly address my question.

Four years ago, when I was eleven, I was raped. I was just walking home and a guy came up behind me and pushed me into his car and took me out in the woods and had some fun. I thought I was ruined for life and no one could ever love me because of what I had done.

Out of shame I never told anyone until a year ago. This was in total confidence. She managed to get me to talk to a friend of hers who is a social worker. Both of them are very good friends of mine now, and I have no choice but to trust them, something I'm not very good at. Unfortunately, neither of them is a Christian, and I have begun to take the attitude that I am going to God only because I want someone to forgive me for what I've done.

But I do not feel very forgiven, probably just because of my stubbornness, since I am sure (or at least I hope) he has forgiven me. But nobody seems to be able to tell me what people like me are supposed to do. The guy had a very sharp knife (I still have scars on my chest), and I'm supposed to keep my virginity? I didn't choose what happened, I didn't want it to happen, and because of it at least one year of my life was literally wiped out. This last summer I got very upset at someone and wanted to do something that would hurt him very badly if he learned about what had happened to me, and I figured I had nothing to lose in that department. I spent three months in torture because I was too ashamed of myself to ask someone to help me find out if I was pregnant. Never again.

I'm not even sure what I'm trying to ask, I just know

that I have to ask and find out soon before I completely give up on trying to live a Christian life. Please be straight with me. I am very tired of circle answers, and I really can't stand to try to find an answer out of another philosophy filled with sympathy or with complete disgust with me. I just need someone with an honest, unprejudiced attitude who won't completely condemn me.

A: I think you are asking whether God condemns you—whether since you're not a virgin, you can ever be worth anything in God's sight (or your own) again. The answer is that God does not condemn you. He never did. What happened was not your fault. You were not the sinner. You were the one sinned against. It was a tragedy, and you have to deal with its consequences, but you *don't* need to deal with guilt over it.

Evidently you do have to deal with guilt feelings. That's very common for people who have been raped or sexually abused. They blame themselves. Sometimes they "act out" their guilt feelings through sexual promiscuity. That's a major reason why counseling is so important for those who have been raped or sexually abused. They need an experienced counselor to work through some of the aftershocks. I'm very glad you told a friend, and I'm even more glad that she got you to a social worker. I only wish you had had that help much sooner.

You mentioned that you have begun to believe you are going to God only because you want forgiveness for what you've done. Let me put that in slightly different language. You don't need someone to forgive you for being raped. You do need someone who knows all about you, yet loves and accepts you unconditionally. It's probably very easy for you to feel rejected. It's probably very easy for you to break up relationships because you're angry. This is a period of your life where you may feel a great deal of hatred toward yourself and toward others. In this period of your life, you need unqualified love—not sympathy, but deep, heartfelt acceptance and appreciation. That's not a bad reason to go to God. He's the only one on earth who can love you as you need to be loved. He wants you to come to him for that love. He's eager to give it.

It may be that your social worker can't understand your need for God. If so, it's important that you find an additional counselor who does understand it. If your social worker is good at her work, she'll help you find such a counselor. You've lost a lot in the past few years. You don't need to add the loss of your relationship with God.

I was sexually abused. Can I ever be healed of these terrible thoughts?

Q: When I was younger my father sexually abused me. At first he forced or threatened me. Later I started giving in because he would act as though he hated me if I didn't, and I wanted so much for him to love me.

A year ago I became a Christian. I love God very much and try to be a good Christian. But I have a problem I cannot control: I am plagued by evil, vulgar thoughts. I'm very ashamed and think they stem from what happened between my father and me.

My mind is in constant turmoil. I once heard that you cannot help what pops into your mind—you're just not supposed to yield to those thoughts. I try to rid myself of them, but they won't stop. I have prayed to God for help and have asked for forgiveness, but I'm not sure that he has forgiven me. I don't deserve forgiveness, but I find it hard to grasp that he won't forgive me when I love him.

A: I'm sure God has already forgiven you. The Bible tells us that anyone who calls on him will be saved (Romans 10:13). I really don't think your problem is with God so much as with your father; and that problem is a big source of confusion in how you think of your Father in heaven.

Quite a number of girls face the same incest problem you did. Some fathers (or uncles, older brothers, or family friends) do molest young girls. And it nearly always has deep psychological effects on the girl. She often feels guilty since she "let" that person do it. I would strongly recommend that you get psychological counseling from a Christian professional. If you ask your pastor where you can find this kind of help, he ought to be able to recommend someone, without spreading the word that you have a problem. You don't even have to tell him what the problem is; just say that you need a professional counselor for a personal matter. If he probes, you can just repeat yourself: it's a personal matter that you want to discuss only with a professional counselor.

There are no magical solutions to your problem. It goes very deep into your thinking, and such thinking can usually be changed only over a long period of time through self-understanding, the love of God and other people, and prayer. But yes, there is hope. Many have overcome this problem and have become more sensitive and helpful to others because they did. Don't feel guilty because you can't overcome it alone; no one can. With help, though, and with time, patience, and love, you can and will beat it.

I was sexually abused. I don't know whether I can trust anyone ever again.

Q: For a long time now I have had a terrible problem. When I was seven years old, I was terribly abused sexually, and a trusted person took my virginity. For eight years I kept this a secret, and I lost many years of childhood because of it. I felt guilty. Then, when I started flunking school, I decided to tell someone. I told a counselor and she put me with social workers who could help me. Even to this day I feel bad sometimes because I have always wanted to wait until marriage for sex; I wanted my husband to have what I can only give the first time once. I am terribly worried about this. What if my husband-to-be doesn't understand?

Last year I had another incident where a much older man tried to make the moves on me. I just froze up. I wanted to stop him, but I just kept thinking about that other time and I couldn't move. Luckily a friend saved me. I see that man often and I become terribly afraid. I am not afraid of all men, but I fear being touched by a man. I have not dated with guys in my school because I'm afraid they might try something and I'll freeze up. I am not a true Christian, but I feel that becoming closer to God will help me. Please give me advice. I am scared. Is it wrong for me to be afraid, to not trust God?

A: Fear and lack of trust are normal responses to what you've been through. You're not at fault any more than a kid who nearly drowns is wrong to fear water. You've shown plenty of courage in letting others in on your secret and getting counseling help. That's an essential beginning.

Now you need to go on to complete healing. You're on the right track when you say that becoming closer to God will help you. You need encouragement, love, and support. God wants to give these. He won't walk out on you. His love is unconditional. He told Joshua that he would never leave or forsake him (Deuteronomy 31:6). He says the same to anyone who follows him today.

A girl wrote me recently, telling me how her step-father had repeatedly molested her as a child. She described how guilty she felt, believing that she was to blame for this horrible situation. She thought if she told anyone, she would be hated for it.

"Through the years a lot has happened," she wrote. "But one thing God convinced me of was that I am a pure and spotless lamb. I am forgiven forever! Jesus Christ loves me and will never, never leave my side. God can heal anyone's life who will submit totally to him. I believe this because of how he has restored my life to be a testimony to others."

I'd encourage you to commit your life to God and begin to ask him for help. That's what a "true Christian" is all about: not a wonderful, moral person, but someone who puts her life in God's hands.

Have you lost something that can never be replaced? Not really. You can't escape being marked by your experience. But "marked" is not the same as "damaged." Take marriage, for example. It's obvious from your letter that your past has affected your feelings about men. Not every man could handle that, but you aren't going to marry every man. You are going to marry only one man, and I trust he will be a wonderfully sensitive person. You will need a husband who is strong and sensitive, who can provide loving reassurance and tenderness. He may need plenty of patience as you work through your fears. There are men with such qualities. If and when you marry one, you'll know you haven't missed anything irreplaceable. In a way, you've gained.

No experience in life is beyond God's working for good. As Romans 8:28 says, "In all things God works for the good of those who love him." Your husband should be the kind of guy who can see the good things God has done in some difficult "things." If he is that kind, he won't regret what you lost. He will be thankful for the sensitive person you have become through the experience.

Of course it would be lovely to enter marriage without any past experiences to regret. That would be, indeed, a gift to your husband. You can bring a different set of gifts, however: the special sensitivity, courage, and faith that we find in those who have been healed of a deep wound.

You're going to need continued and long-term counseling. I'd strongly encourage you to seek it out.

You're also going to need to develop some normal

friendships with men, so that you begin to see them as individuals and not images of the men who have used you. The nonromantic context you'll find in school clubs or church youth groups would be particularly helpful. And as far as the man who put the moves on you is concerned—avoid being alone with him. You don't need the discomfort and fear that he brings.

15. Guilt and Forgiveness

How can I feel God's forgiveness and go on to make a fresh start?

Q: Your magazine makes me feel bad. I feel bad enough just knowing I do wrong every time I'm with my fiancé, but I feel worse when I read what you say. There's nothing I can do to change my past.

One contributing factor to my "messed-up" life was that I never really got along with my father. He always found some reason to criticize me or beat me for some behavior not acceptable to his standards.

Next, dating took its toll. I had my first boyfriend. He talked about marriage. We were only fifteen. I wouldn't give him what he wanted because I was a "Christian." But one night he got me back. I didn't know it was rape until I talked with my mother. So I was fifteen and scared. Counselors and shrinks. . . .

Following that came other events, rather radical for a "Christian girl." To put it briefly, drugs, alcohol, sex. Dropping out of church for the sake of friends and having sex to make up for mistakes that I made with my father.

I've met a man, a wonderful man, who's forgiven me for my past, but yet I haven't forgiven myself. I still see all of it as my fault! My fiancé and I are getting married in three months. Guilt surrounds us. We are trapped! We have not been pure, partly my doing. I forced him to comply with what I wanted. We can't go back. And we have tried to quit, but to no avail. We have failed so many times! Who stays pure? Who can do it? I do not know of any of my Christian friends my age (twenty) who are still virgins.

Can you tell me how to get rid of the guilt of past sexual sins? I want to get my life together *before* I get married. I want to at least establish some kind of halfway mark to ridding myself of this five-year horror story. Please try to sympathize with my story. I come to you as my last hope. I've tried God, I've tried counselors, and I've tried drugs. I've almost stopped trying.

A: When people talk about guilt, they may mean two distinct things. One is a fact: you did something that was wrong, and the penalty hangs over your head. The other is a feeling: a "guilty conscience." In a courtroom, they are interested only in the fact of guilt. Did you or did you not have three drinks before getting into your car? They don't care how you feel. In a psychiatrist's office, on the other hand, they usually are mainly interested in one's feelings.

Ideally, the fact and the feeling should go together. When you do something wrong, you should feel guilty. When the guilt is paid for or forgiven, the feeling should go away. But for many people, the two are out of harmony. People sometimes feel guilt even when they are not factually guilty, or, conversely, they feel no guilt when they really ought to.

How do you stop feeling guilty? Counselors or psychologists will often offer three insights. First, they want you to see that whatever you did is a common weakness. "Don't be so hard on yourself. You're only human." They want you to stop singling yourself out as the worst sinner in the world and to see that you are probably no worse than normal.

Second, they want you to see that whatever you did was shaped by other people and thus not all your fault. For instance, your relationships with your father and your first boyfriend were terribly flawed, and you tried to make up for them through some unwise behavior. Counselors want you not to blame yourself for your father's failings. When you write, "I haven't forgiven myself. I still see it as all my fault," you reflect that view, implying that if you could see it as partly others' fault, you would forgive yourself and not feel so guilty.

Third, they want you to see that while what you did was bad, you didn't do it intending bad. You had other motives. For instance, when you went to bed with various men perhaps you were "trying to make up for what your father failed to give you"—a very good motive, really. In other words, you meant well; you just made some mental miscalculations.

These three insights may be very helpful to you, and there is nothing anti-Christian in them. A Christian would want you to stop blaming yourself as the worst sinner in the world, to understand other people's influence on what you did, and to clarify your own motives. However, from a Christian point of view these insights skip over a principal issue. They address the feelings of guilt, but not the fact of guilt. No matter how many other people do things as bad as you did, no matter who else influenced your action, and no matter how good your motives were, you have done some things that are wrong, and you were and are responsible for it. This fact of guilt is the chief reason why you feel guilty. You have to deal with the fact as well as the feeling.

Many people deny that there is such a thing as real, factual guilt. They believe only in the guilt feelings. Therefore curing guilt is, to them, a question of changing your perspective. The main thing is to "forgive yourself"—by which they mean, usually, forget about whatever you've done.

Christians say that there is a fact of guilt in each person's life, a fact that cannot be forgotten. Christians say this fact will ultimately destroy the person completely by cutting him off from God, the only source of life. If someone has merely forgotten his guilt, a psychologist may consider him healthy but a Christian sees him standing on the brink of destruction. A Christian's first interest is to awaken in him a realization of the fact that he is guilty. Until this fact is confessed and forgiven by God, the person's life is hopeless no matter how good he feels. A Christian's first focus is not on forgiving himself or herself. A Christian focuses on the forgiveness of God.

Here I have some wonderful news to tell you. In Jesus, the *fact* of sin is easy for you to deal with. I did not say easy to deal with, but easy *for you* to deal with. The fact of sin cost God the life of his only Son. Your five-year horror story is well known to Jesus; he felt every bit of it—and died for it. Jesus died to absorb the full nightmare impact of sin and to destroy its power.

The fact of guilt now has no power to destroy your life if you live in Jesus. "If we claim to be without sin, we deceive ourselves and the truth is not in us. If we *confess* our sins, he is faithful and just to forgive us our sins and purify us from all unrighteousness" (1 John 1:8–9). Because of this, and only because of this, you can hope to get out of the trap of guilt.

But I am sure you have confessed your sin to God. What is it, then, that is destroying your life? What seems to be destroying you is the impact of guilt on your personality. Your feeling of "old guilt" would gradually fade away with Jesus' forgiveness, except that you keep renewing it. Your experiences of guilt have deeply affected you. You are stuck in a rut that leaves no room for God's life at all. Every time you sin in the same old way, the feeling of guilt returns and grows stronger. You have been taken over by it instead of by God's Spirit. I call it a feeling of guilt, but it is more than a passing emotion. It is a deep disease making a fundamental difference in every area of your life.

You cannot continue to live in this cycle and experience the real life of Christ. "No one who is born of God will continue to sin, because God's seed remains in him; he cannot go on sinning, because he has been born of God" (1 John 3:9). The apostle John is not talking about occasional failure, which we all have. He refers to a lifestyle of sin. Life with God is incompatible with the way you are living, as unlikely to last as snowballs in June.

So what does this prove? That you are a lost cause? Not at all. It proves that God wants you to change.

Think about the famous story of the woman caught in

adultery (John 8:1–11). A group of religious people brought her to Jesus to hear what he would say about her. They wanted Jesus to agree with them about her guilt and the proper biblical penalty. Unquestionably, they read the Bible correctly—the Old Testament penalty for adultery was death. Jesus did not question that the woman was factually guilty. Instead, he questioned the men's right to condemn her. And he, who had every right, would not condemn her. Rather than death, he gave her freedom.

Yet Jesus' final words leave no doubt that she had to change: "Go now and leave your life of sin."

That is what you need to do.

For you to leave your cycle of guilt, you need first to recognize the reality of Jesus' unlimited forgiveness of your guilt. The basic source of the guilt cycle has been broken. You no longer need to feel guilty or to act as if you are guilty. Jesus does not condemn you.

More than a change in the facts is required, however. A change in your feelings—in your inner self—is required. This will come only as you see yourself making progress away from the guilt cycle you are engaged in.

But is it possible to change? Yes, it is. You ask whether there are any virgins left in the world. Yes, there are. I hear from them all the time. I don't have any statistics on them, but that doesn't really matter because we don't decide how to act by taking a poll. Even in our sexually crazed society some have chosen to wait for marriage. They have had the strength to do that. Even more significant, there are people who have chosen to wait for sexual fulfillment in marriage from now on, regardless of their past failings. The main dividing line in God's view is not between virgins and nonvirgins, but between those who are children of God and those who are not. God's children aren't marked by a history of never doing anything wrong. They are marked as those who have accepted God's forgiveness and committed themselves to following him. A great many people with histories worse than yours are doing that very successfully. They have broken the cycle of sin and guilt.

Perhaps the most important factor in making a change is the realization that change is possible. Neither your past nor your upbringing control you. Your past is powerful, but the Spirit of God is more powerful. God guarantees you this freedom: "God is faithful; he will not let you be tempted beyond what you can bear. But when you are tempted, he will also provide a way out so that you can stand up under it" (1 Corinthians 10:13).

Naturally when you think of escaping your sins, you think in terms of absolute and complete escape, once and for all. Very rarely is the changed life experienced in just those terms. There is not a Christian alive who always resists temptation. All of us fall sometimes. If a person gives up one sin completely, say, drunkenness, he may not immediately even recognize another sin, say, greed. I believe God's chief concern is progress—that you begin to move away from your guiltiness and toward him. You may succeed for a month and then completely break down for a week. The week does not wipe out the month. If that month was lived in real fellowship with God, it was all to the good. You pick yourself up from the week and get back to business.

Even the continual attempt to break free from your pattern is a sign of God's life in you. I thank God you have not been able to rationalize what you have been doing. You still long for the life you know is right. Your persistent agony is itself a sign of God's work in you. Your persistence in seeking purity will, I believe, end in victory.

Not long ago I was trying to break down some concrete steps with a ten-pound sledge hammer. I had thought that concrete would quickly shatter. But it didn't. It took a lot longer than I had planned. Similarly, patterns of sexuality do not shatter quickly; they are much more solid than people think.

I found out, as I hammered those steps, that I am a lot weaker than I had thought. After slamming down the hammer a hundred times or more, my arms felt like chicken fat. My hands would hardly uncurl from the handle. Similarly, when

LOVE, SEX & THE WHOLE PERSON

you resist temptation, you soon realize that you are not so strong as you imagined. You will need help.

Yet I kept hammering. Sometimes my hammering had immediate effect: concrete broke off in big pieces. Other times, though, I would hit the same section again and again and make no perceptible dent. Cement dust flew up, chips of rock zinged out, but the steps stood unmoved. Then, suddenly, I saw a thin crack spreading through them. The accumulated force of many blows had shattered their cohesion. Then, with a few light hits, they broke apart.

Similarly, in trying to break out of a guilt cycle you may feel you are making no progress at all. You wish for a sudden breakthrough, and you grow exhausted trying for one. You are tempted to quit. You see no progress. If you persist, though, you may find that your apparently fruitless efforts were not really fruitless. Imperceptibly you were shattering the basis of the habit. One day it simply breaks apart.

How should you hammer at the habits? I recommend that you read an excellent book on this subject—*Sexual Sanity* by psychologist Earl Wilson. He offers very practical suggestions for breaking sexual compulsions. Here are some:

1. *Recognizing that temptation is mainly mental, analyze the pattern of thoughts and events that leads you to sin.* Often you find a long train that may have begun hours or even days before. When you and your fiancé go out on a date, trouble may begin with the clothes you choose to wear, or the place you choose to go, or even the lack of a plan for the evening! Then you follow a familiar pattern of events; you grow gradually weaker until you finally arrive where you didn't want to be.

You have to derail the train before it really gets going. Early on, when your thoughts are beginning to turn to temptation, you must learn to say "Stop!" to yourself, and substitute some other train of thought. Changing your activity will help. If you're sitting together, get up and take a walk. If you're watching TV, turn it off and read the Bible. If your feelings are turning steamy, sing out loud. Forceful action early on is far more likely to have effect than any efforts to stop the train already beginning to pick up speed. Every time you do what is right you give a hammer blow to that cycle of guilt.

2. *Take responsibility.* That means not blaming God or your parents for what you do and not crying because it seems impossible to live up to the standard you want to live up to. These are ultimately self-pitying thoughts and only half the truth. It is true you are affected by your environment. It is indeed hard to control your life. But you are still the one who can choose to do or not to do anything. Substitute thoughts that emphasize your ability to do right. "I can do everything through him who gives me strength" (Philippians 4:13).

3. *Develop positive relationships.* Often sexual obsession is an attempt to make up for intimacy you missed and badly want—a good relationship with your father, for instance, or really intimate relationships with people of the opposite sex. Sex never makes up for these—in fact it often makes their absence more noticeable. But it will be easier to see and believe that fact when you have loving nonsexual relationships. If you are building a deep relationship with your fiancé, that is a very promising sign. For the good of your marriage, you need to learn to resist temptation together. Friendships with others besides your fiancé will help you put your relationship in perspective and will help you not to expect all your needs to be filled through him. A deepening and joyful relationship with God may help most of all. Get off the guilt track with God and begin to build up your enjoyment of his personality.

4. *Be accountable to someone.* Psychiatrists and counselors can help you understand why you do something, but they do not always provide accountability the way that a trusted friend will. If you can find the courage to entrust your needs to a friend who will not be shocked, but who will listen and pray for you and even check up on you regularly, this will help immensely. The mere fact that you are committed to admitting your sins to someone who cares about you and wants to see you change can give you greater commitment to change.

I would add this: Don't waste time hating yourself. No

matter how much determination you have to change, you will undoubtedly mess up. Such failure will tempt you to feel disgust for yourself. Don't. It doesn't help you. Jesus died for your sins; don't feel you have to kill yourself. Take the attitude that Jesus showed: "Neither do I condemn you. Go now and leave your life of sin."

I have messed up sexually. How can I start growing again?

Q: When I first became a Christian almost six years ago, I met another new Christian—a guy named Sal. We became very strong, active, and involved Christians together. We are on the same wave length.

Then we became separated for three years. When we finally met again (at college), we talked about our lives. A very strange thing has happened. We have both fallen from our close relationship with God. Sex was the reason in both our cases.

Over the years, instead of growing as Christians, we regressed. We both expressed the same feeling of utter disgust with our lack of ability to control our sex drives. Our continual pleas to God and our continual failures have led to more and more erosion of our relationship with God.

I will not go into detail concerning our sexual exploits. But let it suffice to say Sal was seduced by a girl who had asked him out. And I had a similar experience with my past girlfriend who I thought was a very strong Christian. I have since broken up with this girl even though I still have very strong feelings for her. Sal also broke his engagement.

But our relationships with God are still not good. I am trying to read the Bible, pray regularly, and get involved with fellowship. I have also resumed my involvement with a Christian organization similar to Big Brother. I am trying to abstain from any involvement with girls and dating. But things are not good for Sal or for me. Our attitudes are poor; our faith in God has deteriorated. Society has taught us well that beauty and well-built bodies are the things to look for in girls. Our eyes and hormones reaffirm this.

So where are we now? Back to where we started, with a lot of growing to do. I don't mean to be so negative and unpleasant, but Sal and I are not happy with what has happened to our lives. We realize we are to blame, but that doesn't help much. So if you have any ideas on how to start our regrowth, we would be most appreciative.

A: I think you are going in the right direction. You have grasped the danger in the way you've been going, and you sound sincere in wanting to change. Getting back into fellowship, reading the Bible, and doing Christian work may feel like "going through the motions," but going through the motions is essential when you're trying to regain your form.

You should find the book of Hebrews helpful reading. It was addressed to people who were both discouraged about their Christian life and tempted to make it simply a ritual. The writer to the Hebrews basically stresses three things. He does not urge his discouraged readers to go out and try to work miracles. He says:

1. *They should think deeply about the facts of the Gospel, so that they can realize again how wonderful God's salvation is.* Your study of the Bible should concentrate on this: not getting an emotional high but grappling with an understanding of just what God has done for you.

2. *The writer also says they should persist—they should "hang in there."* He warns against the dreadful consequences of not doing so. Many people go through a wilderness at some time in their lives. But the way out of any wilderness is not to sit down and give up. The way out is to continue day by day in the direction you know is right.

3. *The writer encourages the Hebrews to think about the great men and women of faith and to imitate their lives.* You

might do this by doing a Bible study on the lives of some of them—for example, Abraham, Joseph, Rahab, David, Daniel, and Jeremiah. And people of faith aren't found only in the Bible. There may be some near you. Seek them out and imitate their pattern of life. When you are discouraged, you particularly need fellowship with mature, hopeful people whom you can respect—those who have had experience in life and have come through with flying colors.

I don't think I need to tell you that you must avoid getting sexually involved again. You need some positive experience with girls (though you may be right to simply stay away from dating for a while). You also need some positive experiences with yourself, discovering that you can be sexually attracted to someone without losing control.

Stay away from situations where temptation is going to be strong. Many people seem to go wrong in a bedroom very late at night with someone they knew (or suspected, anyway) was on the make. And then they act surprised.

The God who says, "I will never leave you nor forsake you" will show you the way, if you ask. There is hardly a Christian who does not, at some time in his life, go through a failure phase that leaves him deeply discouraged. But if you persist in faith and try to grow to a deeper understanding of God, this struggle will be only a phase. You will emerge stronger and wiser—and more deeply appreciative of God's grace.

I know God forgives me, but I can't forgive myself!

Q: Last year in October I started going with a guy who was twenty-nine years old (I was seventeen), and I really fell for him. We went out a couple of times. We kissed, but never did any heavy petting. He would try, but I'd always stop him.

Then in November he told me he didn't know how long he could go on like that, and if I loved him I'd have sex with him. I didn't want to, but he said in so many words that if I didn't, we were through. So I did have sex in order not to lose him. I'm still regretting it.

You see, I was raised to believe you're not to have sex until you're married, but the thing I really hate myself for is the fact that I did not enjoy it. He'd get very passionate, but I couldn't. (I began to think something was wrong with me.)

We had sex only five times before I started making excuses not to, and finally we just drifted apart. I'm very embarrassed when I see him now. I've asked God to forgive me and I believe he has. But how do I forgive myself? How do I stop hating myself and get rid of this embarrassment?

A: God forgives us once and for all, but you have to forgive yourself repeatedly. You will just have to be tough and refuse to give in to the feelings when they come up. Tell yourself, "I will not go on punishing myself as though somehow that will make up for what I did. God has forgiven me; there is no reason to dwell on this." Ask God to help you put those self-hating thoughts out of your mind and remind you of how much he loves you. Then go on and get busy doing something else.

If you consistently refuse to pity yourself, those ugly feelings will gradually go away. It takes time. In the meantime, thank God that his forgiveness isn't as up and down as ours.

What if I don't feel any guilt at all?

Q: I'm an eighteen-year-old girl and a nine-year-old Christian. Christ knows me thoroughly, and I learn more about him every day as I read the Bible and spend quiet times with him. But there's one particular area I simply don't know how to give over to him. My physical body is a big, big stumbling block in my road to making him Lord.

Why did God have to make our bodies so enticingly beautiful? Not only am I in the trap of vanity about my own body, but I am also very enslaved to the male bodies in my life.

I do know the value of a good friendship with someone of the opposite sex, because I've had male friends who were even closer than almost all my female friends. And I know also, by experience, that sex sometimes gets in the way of good friendships.

But there are some men in my life that I simply don't hold back from. It's not because I'm afraid of losing them. It's just that I have desires equal to theirs, and I hate frustration.

The problem is I just don't feel the conviction and guilt that "nice Christian girls" are all supposed to automatically feel when guys get closer than a foot away!

Can this be corrected or am I simply a lost cause? Guilt is not my problem—it's the lack of guilt that intrigues me.

A: I am sure you are not a lost cause. But you're not an easy cause, either. A sensitive conscience is a gift that God offers to help people want to do the things they know are right and to give them no peace until they stop doing the things they know are wrong. Apparently in the area of sex, your conscience isn't working very well. There might be a lot of reasons for that. It could be your doing; if you violate your conscience often enough, it quits. Or maybe you're the result of our world's declining morals—your conscience has been "educated" by too many sex-loaded giggles on TV or by too many isn't-adultery-beautiful movies.

It's hard to change when your conscience doesn't motivate you. But nowhere did Jesus say, "Let your conscience be your guide." He was much more interested in letting God's Word be your guide. If your conscience doesn't prod you, how about your respect for God?

Your letter leaves me with the impression that you're not taking this problem terribly seriously. You're "intrigued" by your lack of guilt. But you're still laughing a little at "nice Christian girls."

God doesn't consider it a laughing matter. Listen to what Paul wrote in 1 Corinthians 6:9–10: "Do not be deceived: Neither the sexually immoral, nor idolaters, nor adulterers . . . will inherit the kingdom of God." Galatians 5:19–21 puts the same message just as strongly. The writing is on the wall; you cannot continue as you have been doing. Either you will lose God or you will lose your sins. With or without the help of your conscience, it is your responsibility.

But it is not your responsibility alone. That passage in 1 Corinthians goes on to say, "And that is what some of you were. But you were washed, you were sanctified, you were justified in the name of the Lord Jesus Christ and by the Spirit of our God." Galatians 5:22 similarly goes on to list the fruit of the Spirit in a person's life, and this fruit includes self-control.

I would, if I were you, ask God to give you a sense of the deep life-and-death consequences of these issues. And then ask to be filled with his Spirit, who will give you the strength to do what is right and teach you in the deepest part of your being what you already know in your head—that you are doing wrong. Make that your prayer, and keep on praying it until it begins to make a difference in your life.

Should I "tell all" to my new love?

Q: Three years ago I had my first steady girlfriend. I was a little on the shy side, while she was quite aggressive. She initiated all our sexual activity. I hardly knew her, and I knew I didn't love her, but she was nice and attractive. We dated three months and then she decided she wanted to go out with other guys, so we broke up.

What I'm writing about is that today, three years later, I am in love with a sweet and caring Christian girl. I did things with my first girlfriend that I feel very dirty and guilty about. I'm sorry and have asked the Lord to forgive me, and I know he has, but I still feel dirty inside.

Should I tell my new girlfriend about it? We do *nothing* like that and we've been going out for two years. How do I get rid of the bad feelings I have inside?

A: In the military, especially in wartime, secret information is disclosed according to a rule known as "need to know." You apply it by asking this question: To carry out his duties, does this person need to know this information? If not, he shouldn't be told.

How much your girlfriend needs to know depends a lot on how serious you are in your relationship. In a casual relationship, I don't think she needs to know anything. At the other extreme, when two people are making definite plans for marriage, I think they should know all that they want to know. Married people don't keep secrets, I believe.

Since you've been going together for two years, I'd imagine you're fairly serious. Probably your girlfriend is at least aware that there's something in your past making you uncomfortable. It could be interfering with the ease you have in relating to her. If so, I'd think she should know enough to help her understand what's affecting you today. You might say something like this:

"I think you need to know that three years ago I got involved with a girl, and we went farther sexually than we should have. I deeply regret that, and I've asked God to forgive me for it, but some bad memories are still there. Maybe you've been sensing that at times. Those memories are one reason I'm so thankful for our relationship, which has been free from such problems. I'd appreciate your prayers for me that those memories will be healed."

As to getting rid of the bad feelings, I know of three aids. First, and most important, is time. I'd imagine you feel as though you've already given it plenty of time. Yet sexual experiences touch the core of our existence, and memories of them fade very, very slowly. They do fade, however. In time, I promise, they won't be troubling you.

That's assuming you have the second aid: a healing environment. The fact that you've had a positive, healthy relationship with another girl for two years is a very good sign. I hope you're also able to get together with some Christian guys, to encourage each other and pray for each other. Ideally, you'll also have an older friend who can counsel you. Just sharing your past problems with such a person would help free you.

The third aid is the forgiveness of God. It's there, and you know it's there. Often it doesn't immediately penetrate to all the levels of feeling. Still, the important fact is that you have been forgiven. You have a new start. Let me refer you to 2 Corinthians 5:17—"If anyone is in Christ, he is a new creation; the old has gone, the new has come!" You may not feel entirely new, but you are. Given enough time and a healing environment, that fact will turn your feelings around.

How can I forgive my love's past sexual mistakes?

Q: I am twenty years old, and I am a virgin. I have been dating my boyfriend for about two years. A couple of months into the relationship he told me he wasn't a virgin. I understood and accepted it then. Now it is finally hitting me. We are both Christians, and we plan on getting married in a few years. I've forgiven him for what he did, yet I am having a hard time struggling with this. I love him very much, yet sometimes I think that our honeymoon won't be special because of what he did. I have prayed about it and have tried to forget about it, and I'm still confused. My question is, should this really bother me as much as it does, and if not, how can I stop it from bothering me?

A: Yes, it should bother you. The current idea that sex is a pleasant get-acquainted exercise for potential lovers would suggest that nothing very big happened between your boyfriend and his nameless bedmate of the past. But that's not true. Sex is the deepest, most intimate exchange two people can make. It affects them deeply, and they carry the memories for the rest of their lives—good or bad. So naturally, you are bothered to know that someone you love has been to bed with someone else.

That's not the same, however, as saying that your boyfriend's past has to ruin your future together. The past can't be ignored or undone, but it can be *forgiven*. Forgiveness is a mystery, really—a grace that God alone can give us. I don't know how to tell you to forgive your boyfriend, and to get that forgiveness to penetrate to the bottom of this barrier. But I do believe it's what needs to happen for your relationship to go forward. You need to fully confront what happened and the pain it caused—and then ask God for his help in covering it over with love.

If you love your boyfriend deeply enough, that love will enable you to forgive—not ignoring the pain he's brought you but weaving it into a bigger fabric of your relationship so that ultimately you are tied together more strongly than ever. If that happens, your honeymoon will be, indeed, very special—not special in just the same way it would have been if you both were virgins, but special in its own way—flooded with the depth of your forgiveness and love for him.

My girlfriend told me about her past. I'm having a hard time handling my reaction.

Q: In a couple of past issues you counseled two different girls about telling their boyfriend/husband about previous sexual experiences. I fully agree with you about the need for them to do so. What a shock it would be if your wife told you of her past after marriage.

But my problem is that a girl I love did tell me about her past. I have done a lot of praying about God's design for our relationship and my handling of this situation. I respect her for having the honesty to tell me of her past, and I love her too much to cause her the pain that I know it would bring if I told her of my anguish. I guess the base of my problem comes from the high standard I set for myself in keeping from sex until marriage.

In a way I am bitter because she didn't keep the same standards. I once told her that though it was God who had to forgive her, I forgave her also. But sometimes I wonder if I did. Am I being a prude, or unfair to her? Please tell me outright. I know that the experiences she had were one-night stands, that she didn't love the guys involved, and that the experiences came during a crisis in her life when she had run away from home. (Would I have been able to do better under the circumstances?) Most important, she really was not a Christian at the time. I love this girl, and she loves me. I'm thinking of asking her to be my wife. Will these doubts of mine cause us problems we won't be able to handle? Should I tell her of the hassle in my mind?

A: I don't find it terribly surprising that you're reacting the way you are. Some people aren't bothered at all by the past life of their partner, but many find themselves deeply upset by it. It doesn't follow that you're being a prude. You should feel hurt and troubled to know that the one person you love and want to marry was so troubled and used.

I think you should tell her how you are feeling. If you do marry, you are going to feel many more heartaches, many more jealousies. If you keep them to yourself to protect her, you will cut her off from an opportunity to understand you and comfort you. It's condescending, I think, to assume that she isn't strong enough to handle your feelings.

If you marry, your grief is hers; hers is yours. You might as well find out now whether you can take that kind of intimate sharing. Probably when you tell her how you feel, it will help release your powerful emotions. You may feel worse for a time, and she may feel terribly guilty all over again, but I believe it's likely you can work your way through it. That broken and reknit fragment of your life will become a private bond between you. If it doesn't—if you simply can't share your deepest feelings with each other, good or bad—then you ought to put off marriage until you can.

16. Miscellaneous Topics

Birth control.

It's striking to me that in all the years I've spent answering kids' questions about sex and love, I've seen just one or two questions about birth control. Evidently curiosity is slight.

Yet birth control is the *one* subject many adults want kids to know. If you read materials from, say, the Planned Parenthood Association, it's evident they evaluate effective sex education mostly on the basis of whether kids know how to use condoms.

I haven't been overly concerned with this issue for two reasons. One is that I think kids know where to get condoms and how to use them. You could leave packages of condoms on the front lawn of the high school every morning and run videos on how to use them on TV every night, and I don't think it would make kids use condoms a great deal more than they already do. I don't think it's mainly an information problem. I think it's an attitude problem. Kids who have sex generally don't want to think about being responsible. That's the farthest thing from their minds.

Second, I don't think condoms are the ultimate solution to America's sexual problems. I am concerned, very concerned, about teenage pregnancies, abortions, and sexually transmitted diseases. If everybody used condoms when they had sex, these problems would decrease (though not disappear). Still, deeper problems would persist—the broken relationships, broken families, and broken hearts that are the inevitable consequence of sex outside of marriage. That's why I've argued for abstinence. It's the best way.

It's true, nonetheless, that a lot of kids *do* have sex together. I'm convinced it's the wrong choice, but I know some kids will make that choice. If you do, you certainly ought to use birth control.

I would like to put that even more strongly. If you have sex before marriage, I believe you're making a serious mistake. If you have sex before marriage and don't use birth control, you are crazy. The argument for waiting until marriage is subtle. The argument for birth control is so obvious that even stupid people ought to get it.

The pill is probably the most effective in terms of birth control alone. It's not foolproof—there is no 100 percent effective means of birth control—but it's pretty close. On the negative side, some women do experience side effects. Also, a woman has to get on the pill and stay on it, every day. That requires a lot of consistency, which isn't always the easiest thing for teenagers to provide. Besides all that, the pill offers no protection against sexually transmitted diseases.

There are other options, but the one most people favor today is the condom. It's medically safe. It's easy to get. It's about 90 percent effective in preventing pregnancy. And condoms provide considerable (though far from perfect) protection against AIDS, chlamydia, herpes, genital warts, gonorrhea, syphilis, and other sexually transmitted diseases. Some of these diseases are incurable. Some are curable but hard to detect, so you can get them and never realize it until it's too late.

Some people wonder whether unmarried Christians should even consider birth control, since it shows they are planning to have sex, which they know is wrong. I look at it this way: if you feel you just can't help driving at unsafe speeds, at least do it on lonely roads where you're less likely to hurt other people. It's not the right thing to do, but there's no reason for making the wrong thing worse than it already is.

LOVE, SEX & THE WHOLE PERSON

Oral sex.

Q: I am a seventeen-year-old senior in high school. I am very curious about oral sex. I just recently learned what oral sex actually is. My first impression was, "Oh my gosh, that is the sickest thing I've ever heard of." Then I started thinking that it must not be if you really love the person and if you're married. I'm curious about the Lord's feelings on oral sex and why some Christians refuse to talk about it.

A: Some Christians don't talk about it because they don't see any good in talking about it. Discussing the details of sexual technique can inflame the imagination, and there's not the least bit of help one can get out of it before marriage. It's not just oral sex that people don't like to talk about; they don't talk about any of the varied ways of making love. I agree with that. Sex is an extremely private affair, and I dislike the modern tendency to discuss it as though one is describing football plays.

However, oral sex causes quite a bit of conversation among curious young people, and I doubt that much of such conversation is from a Christian perspective. Let me try to make up for that.

Scripture does not indicate what the Lord thinks of oral sex—or any other sexual technique. God seems less interested in sexual technique than the context in which it is exercised. In loving marriage, anything that both partners want to do, and that isn't harmful or dangerous, they are free to do.

In marriage just about anything goes, but that does not mean everything is required. Lots of people find oral-genital contact "gross." That's just fine. They are under no obligation to try it. This is a matter (like all sexual matters) that is up to a married couple to decide in loving and gentle consideration for each other.

But that's in marriage. Some people have suggested that

since you can't get pregnant through oral sex, and "virginity" is preserved, those who aren't ready for marriage will find it a handy, harmless substitute for intercourse. I think that's nonsense. God's concern for virginity has little to do with the physiology of sex and much to do with the intimacy referred to in the Bible as "knowing" another person. You can't get more intimate than oral sex, and I conclude that for unmarried people it's out of bounds.

How do you cope with the party scene?

Q: I am a seventeen-year-old high school senior and a Christian. I am very confused because I can't live up to the standards set by my parents and Christian peers. I am dating a guy I'll call Ted. Ted is a Christian and very nice. We've known each other for only two months, but I know that I like him very much. Our relationship is a very healthy Christian type, and we haven't gone very far at all—only kissing.

My biggest problem is partying—something Ted can't stand. I don't drink very often, but when I do I usually end up drunk. The past couple of times I've been at a party and gotten drunk, I've ended up making out with this guy I'll call John. John and I are good friends, but when we're both drunk it gets to be more than that. Last night I was at a party. Ted wasn't there, but John was. I got drunk, and John took me in his car to some secluded spot. We ended up having sex. I can't call it making love because love had nothing to do with it. I feel terrible about what happened, cheap and terrible.

I can't talk to anyone about this. None of my Christian friends know I party. My parents would lose all trust in me. I am also worried that I could be pregnant because neither of us used any protection. What can I do?

A: You can't do much about last night. You can pray it over with God and gain a deeper sense of his love and care for you. But praying over the future is probably more important.

There's something still attracting you in the wild life you find at parties. Although you've known for some time that you don't want your life to go in that direction, you obviously haven't totally closed yourself to it. Well, it's time for you to close that door.

Some Christians are strong enough to mix with any crowd and still be themselves. They can be at a wild party and shed light, rather than absorbing darkness. Jesus was that kind of person, and perhaps you will be too someday. Right now you're not. Getting loaded and making out may represent only 5 percent of your life, but that is (as you know) a potent and dangerous 5 percent. I'd recommend you make up your mind to quit partying and drinking and playing around. Don't cut back. Quit completely. Then go and tell some friends about your decision. You don't need to tell them the details of your past, but you can ask them to share the details of your future.

Living a double life is not healthy. Look and pray for a handful of truly confidential friends who will support and help you in your decisions.

We thought we could handle alcohol. We were wrong.

Q: My friend is a guy, and I'm a girl. We were both raised in church and are Christians. All through high school we went to the youth-group meetings and listened to what the youth pastor said, and we agreed with him. There is no doubt in my mind nor my friend's that premarital sex is wrong. We both set high standards and were sure nothing would ever lower them. Yet no one ever told us that something would lower our standards in a flash—namely, alcohol.

My friend and I are great friends, and we never really thought drinking was wrong for us, except because we were under age. He and I used to go drinking together, yet we had no problem because we were just friends. We both felt we could handle drinking.

Well, were we wrong! Dead wrong. One night I went out with some guys who were basically just casual acquaintances, except for one whom I had dated twice. These guys decided to introduce me to the joys of beer. The four of us had a case, which meant six cans per person. I had never had that much to drink before, and *never* before had I drunk on an empty stomach. Needless to say, I got drunk rather rapidly because I was going to keep up with the guys. I didn't, but that's not the point.

The guy I had dated decided to take advantage of my condition, I think. I do not remember anything after the fourth beer, yet when I got home in the morning I was without a bra, and my underwear was inside out. I know in my heart that mentally I am still a virgin, yet I'm no longer one physically.

A somewhat similar experience happened to my friend. He was very depressed, and there was a party at his home, so since he wouldn't have to drive, he didn't care how much he drank. He doesn't remember much of anything except waking up in the morning in his bed, naked with a girl.

We both know that God has forgiven us and that we won't make the same mistake again, but we will always live with the uncertainty of what happened on those nights. It is terrible wondering. With God's help we will be able to overcome those feelings. We just wish someone had told us that drinking takes away resistance. Please, share this problem with others and save them the heartache.

A: We get the message, grim as it is. I've heard a lot from people like you who got drunk and ended up in someone else's bed. In some cases, they were raped; in other instances, the alcohol loosened their inhibitions so that they went along with something they wouldn't do when they were sober; sometimes they simply had no memory of what happened. Regardless of the circumstances, those who got drunk feel horrible.

This world has an awful sickness in it. The virus is everywhere and affects everyone. You never know when you'll be victimized by a stranger, by a friend, or (most commonly of all) by yourself. One thing you can count on, though: wherever there is heavy drinking, you'll find victims.

When is it right to say "I love you"?

Q: I am sixteen years old. My girlfriend is seventeen. We live a few hundred miles away from each other but keep in touch by letters. Every few months we get together. We've had very strong feelings toward each other for a year now and feel Christ has something in store for us both.

My question is: We tell one another that we love each other. Is it right? I know we are still young, but that is the only way we can express what we feel for each other.

A: Saying "I love you" is something like kissing. There's no harm in the thing itself, but it can lead to problems.

First, there are misunderstandings. For some people "I love you" merely means, "I feel powerfully attracted to you." For others, it means, "I want to care for you and put your interests above my own." For still others it virtually means, "You are the one I have chosen to marry." If you are going to say, "I love you," sit down together and talk about just what you mean and don't mean.

Second, "I love you" can be used to manipulate each other. Some guys use it to get girls into bed with them. I'm sure you're not that crass. But there is sometimes the temptation to use those powerful words, not because you mean them, but to affect your partner in some way—to get her to do something you want to do, to calm her down, to keep her with you when she's ready to move on.

Third, like kissing, the words tend to outlive the commitment. It is very common for a couple who are really tired of each other to kiss all the harder, as if they could make up for their loss of love. They may also say "I love you" all the more. It is not bad to work at sticking together, but these are false ways of doing it.

I do not find anything wrong with saying "I love you." But I would try to keep the words precious by using them carefully, preserving their meaning.

How important are appearances and sexual attraction?

Q: I am not trying to sound stuck up when I say that I have good looks. More than a few guys have liked me for my looks. My friends tell me that boyfriends are no trouble for me, but they are. Most guys don't take the time to find out what I'm really like, and that hurts.

I am proud to say that I don't just go out with a guy because he's good looking. I like to find out what he's like and whether or not he's a Christian. Guys that aren't Christians are a big turn-off to me.

Well, the problem is that I have met a guy who means a lot to me now, but he's not the greatest in the looks department. Personally I think he's kind of cute. My friends tell me that I could get a guy who is much better looking and that I should try. The thing is, though, I really like this one and am happy to be just with him. He is a very good Christian and wouldn't even ask me to do anything against God's wishes. What should I do about my friends' pressure on me? I can't take much more of it.

A: Evidently your friends have a pretty immature view of guys. Dating is not a poodle show in which you compete to see who got the prettiest one. Looks are nice, but people in a relationship usually do more than look at each other. Personality and character are far more valuable—and far more enjoyable. If *you* like the way he looks, that's all that matters. Your friends' opinion is irrelevant, unless he wants to ask *them* out.

But how do you turn off the pressure? Usually one or two people control the tempo of a clique. Get them aside, one at a time, and talk about how you're feeling. They'll probably come around.

If they don't, don't worry. The pressure won't last long. It probably sounds loud, but it's not likely to be deep. Once people see that you're serious, that you really like the guy, that you don't care how pretty a poodle he is, they'll switch to another subject.

I'm considered the ugly duckling of my high school.

Q: This has been the loneliest and saddest year of my life. I've never had a boyfriend. I'm considered the ugly duckling of my high school. Guys make fun of the way I walk, talk, breathe, and think. Sometimes I just start crying and can't seem to stop. Every guy I take interest in rejects me; I always end up getting hurt, and the pain just won't go away. This year I met a terrific guy who was really nice to me. He's got a super personality. He used to call me every once in a while. He found out I like him, though, and slowly stopped communicating. I haven't heard from him in weeks.

It hurts me. Some guys can like me for a friend, it seems, but never for a girlfriend. To make matters worse, I have a curved spine and I'll have to have a back brace. Now I feel like I'll never get a date, and I'll be lucky if I can get one guy to look at me as a human being (not a dog).

How can I change things? When I pray and ask God to help me with this certain guy, to bring us closer, it turns out we go farther apart. I can't take much more of this rejection. One of my friends is just like me, and she attempted suicide twice. Please tell me how I can get guys to stop saying how ugly I am and start thinking of me as a possible date.

A: I wish there were magic that would do the trick. If there is, I haven't heard of it yet.

Physical appearance is a tricky thing, though. It has as much to do with clothes and grooming as with the raw material God gave you. One way to stop people from calling you ugly is to stop dressing ugly. You'll need some help with this, I imagine. Is there someone whose style you admire? Could you find the nerve to ask that person for some advice?

But even that isn't enough. If a miracle should turn you into a rare beauty, your problems would be far from solved. The fact is, most people tend to take their opinion of you from your own opinion of yourself. A friend told me an incident that captures that. Robby, the most popular kid in his school, had a new shoe that squeaked. Any other kid would have gone around cringing all day, hoping no one would notice. But Robby loved it. He thought his shoe was the greatest thing happening. He took every excuse to walk up to the teacher's desk, his shoe squeaking. He wasn't just being a clown—he really liked that squeak. And because he liked it, everybody else did too.

What you like about yourself, others will like. What you hate, others will hate. Of course, you can't just make up your mind to like yourself—the patterns of a lifetime don't change easily or quickly. But you can do two things. You can begin talking to God in a new way. Instead of pleading with him for a boyfriend, begin to thank him for what he's given you. Perhaps there are only a few things you're thankful for— thank him for those regularly. Thank him that when everybody else rejects you, he still loves you. Thank him that he has made a new person out of you and that you do have the potential to overcome problems.

Second, find someone to talk to and pray with. A pastor, a Campus Life staff worker, a girlfriend—anyone you trust to make a commitment to stick with you for a set period of time, encouraging you as you make progress. Reaching out to someone like that isn't easy, but it can make a great difference.

None of this solves the problem of how to attract a boyfriend. That's because I don't think it's a problem to solve. Right now a boyfriend would only bring more problems into your life.

But if you learn to love yourself and begin looking for ways to make yourself more attractive, friends, including boyfriends, will come at the proper time. You need to understand your beauty, inward if not outward, so that when you offer yourself to someone, you will have something really worthwhile to offer.

Speaking up for God's perspective with your friends.

Q: I don't know what it's like in other places, but at my school if I ever told people that, say, petting was wrong, I'd be laughed out of the place.

Just once in my health class I tried to stand up against premarital sex, and you would have thought I was out of my mind. Not one other kid agreed with me, and there were even some Christians in the class.

It really bothers me to be standing around with a bunch of my friends, and they start talking about something somebody did at a party or something. It makes me feel terrible, because I feel I should say something and I can't. They'd just make a big joke out of it. What should I do?

A: Standing around in a group probably isn't the best atmosphere for presenting the Christian view of sex. The peer pressure can be pretty heavy. If you want to talk deeply about an issue, you need to get one-on-one with friends. That way they aren't under any pressure, and neither are you.

But there is something to be said for speaking up in the group, too. You have to face the fact that Christians are in the minority in their views on sex, and we have to adopt minority tactics. It doesn't help to be shocked at what people think or to launch into a big harangue. Your attitude should communicate, "I know my beliefs are different, but I also know they're beliefs I can confidently stake my life on."

And when you speak, think of it as planting truth, the way a farmer plants seeds. Don't worry about planting seeds one day and not seeing the results immediately. Give seeds of truth time to grow in other people. Let them get frustrated with their own way of doing things. Let them see that you've got your own life together.

By doing this, you may end up helping other timid Christians, too. One girl told me, "A really outspoken girl helped me. She just wasn't afraid to speak up. After a while people accepted her. She was always positive, and she didn't get angry. She wasn't afraid to admit it when she didn't understand something. She just said what she thought. They didn't try to argue with her; they just respected her position. They knew where she stood. Seeing her, I realized I didn't have to be on the defensive. She helped me to be bold and uncompromising."

Judging People.

Q: How can you keep from judging people when you think they are wrong? In our school there are two teachers who are having an open affair, and everyone just accepts it. Several times someone has said how cool these teachers are, and I've said something in disagreement. One girlfriend, who went to church a lot when she was young, has said every time, "Hey, aren't you judging? I thought your Bible said not to judge." She even showed me the place where Jesus says that. Now my other friends have started saying it, too. Can't I say anything?

A: The other day I cooked some fish that had been in the refrigerator for longer than I had realized. When I tasted it, I had to spit it out. I said, "This fish is rotten." Was I judging the fish?

Or how about a teacher who grades your paper and has to flunk you. Is he judging?

I don't think so. In both these situations you're evaluating. You're comparing the way things are with the way they should be. I'd guess when you say you don't think what your teachers are doing is cool, you're evaluating. You're saying, "According to my beliefs, what they are doing isn't good." The only alternative is acting as though everything anybody ever does or thinks is right—which clearly isn't so.

There is another kind of judging: the kind judges do. They evaluate a situation and say, "This fellow killed that fellow, and I believe that's wrong." But they go beyond that, too. Sooner or later a judge hands out punishment.

Sometimes other people do the same thing. I knew a guy who thought it was wrong for guys to have long hair. He had a right to think that. But he decided he could talk only to fellows with crewcuts! If your hair was long, he couldn't be your friend. That was his "punishment" for those who had a haircut he didn't approve of. That's the kind of judging Jesus was talking about, I believe, when he said, "Do not judge."

Christians are called to love people who disagree with them. That means we speak out and state our views, but we don't "punish" people for disagreeing with us by withdrawing friendship or talking behind their backs.

Let's face it. We're going to be in the minority on a lot of things. It would be easier to behave like a deaf-mute every time you disagree with someone, or to drop friends who don't agree with you. But that isn't what Jesus wants. Anyone, he said, can love someone who's lovable. It's only when people aren't on our side that loving them becomes something special. Obviously, in your case that means the teachers and the friends who don't agree with you.